Chester Frisbie

Behavioral Goals
of
General Education
in
High School

By WILL FRENCH
and Associates

RUSSELL SAGE FOUNDATION
New York   ~   ~   1957

© 1957
RUSSELL SAGE FOUNDATION
Printed in the United States
of America

Library of Congress
Catalog Card Number: 57-12705

WM. F. FELL CO., PRINTERS
PHILADELPHIA, PA.

MEMBERSHIP OF PARTICIPATING COMMITTEES

PLANNING AND EDITORIAL COMMITTEE

J. DAN HULL, Director, Instruction, Organization, and Services, U.S. Office of Education, Washington

NOLAN C. KEARNEY, Assistant Superintendent of Schools for Curriculum and Research, St. Paul, Minnesota

PAUL R. KLOHR, Assistant Dean, College of Education, Ohio State University, Columbus

C. W. SANFORD, Dean of Admissions, University of Illinois, Urbana

HOWARD G. SPALDING, Principal, A. B. Davis High School, Mount Vernon, New York

WILLIAM W. TURNBULL, Executive Vice-President, Educational Testing Service, Princeton, New Jersey

BENJAMIN C. WILLIS, General Superintendent of Schools, Chicago, Illinois

DONALD YOUNG, President, Russell Sage Foundation, New York City

LEONARD S. COTTRELL, JR., Social Psychologist, Russell Sage Foundation

JOHN E. DOBBIN, Educational Testing Service, Project Director

WILL FRENCH, Executive Editor for the project

COMMITTEE OF CONSULTANTS

EDNA P. AMIDON, Chief, Home Economics Education Branch, U.S. Office of Education, Washington

REGINALD F. ARRAGON, Richard F. Scholz Professor of History, Reed College, Portland, Oregon

PRUDENCE BOSTWICK, Professor of Education, Los Angeles State College, California

PAUL F. BRANDWEIN, Associate Director, Joint Council on Economic Education, New York City

T. HARRY BROAD, Director of Instruction and Curriculum, Oklahoma City

DAN H. COOPER, Director, Division of Education, Purdue University, Lafayette, Indiana

WILLIAM H. CORNOG, Superintendent, New Trier High School, Winnetka, Illinois

JOHN J. DE BOER, Professor of Education, University of Illinois, Urbana

HAROLD P. FAWCETT, Professor of Education, Ohio State University, Columbus

ROBERT S. GILCHRIST, Superintendent of Schools, University City, Missouri

HAROLD C. HAND, Professor of Education, University of Illinois, Urbana

LAVONE A. HANNA, Professor of Education, San Francisco State College, California

ROBERT J. HAVIGHURST, Chairman, Committee on Human Development, University of Chicago, Illinois

J. PAUL LEONARD, President, American University, Beirut, Lebanon

CAMILLA M. LOW, Professor of Education, University of Wisconsin, Madison

MORRIS MEISTER, Principal, The Bronx High School of Science, New York City

WILLIAM J. MICHEELS, Chairman, Department of Industrial Education, University of Minnesota, Minneapolis

AILEEN SCHOEPPE, Associate Professor of Education, New York University

5

COMMITTEE OF ADVISERS

MARGARET ARMSTRONG, Member, New Jersey State Board of Education, Stewartsville

HODDING CARTER, Editor, Delta Democrat-Times, Greenville, Mississippi

NORMAN COUSINS, Editor, The Saturday Review, New York City

GEORGE H. GALLUP, Director, American Institute of Public Opinion, Princeton, New Jersey

O. H. ROBERTS, JR., President, National School Boards Association, Evansville, Indiana

DAEL WOLFLE, Director, American Association for the Advancement of Science, Washington

COMMITTEE OF REVIEWERS

MARCILLENE BARNES, Director of Instruction, Grand Rapids Public Schools, Michigan

MELVIN W. BARNES, Superintendent of Schools, Oklahoma City

CLIFFORD S. BARTHOLOMEW, Principal, Allentown High School, Allentown, Pennsylvania

VIRGINIA CASEY, English and Common Learnings Department, Lakeview High School, Decatur, Illinois

ELEANOR CROUCH, Curriculum Coordinator, Carmel Unified School District, Carmel-By-The-Sea, California

NELDA DAVIS, Supervisor of Secondary Social Studies, Houston Independent School District, Texas

LOIS DILLEY, Head, English Department, West Senior High School, Rockford, Illinois

JEAN FAIR, Testing and Research, Evanston Township High School, Evanston, Illinois

SAUL GEFFNER, Chairman, Department of Science, Forest Hills High School, New York

FLORENCE C. GUILD, Editor for High School English, Ginn and Company, Boston, Massachusetts

JOE HALL, Associate Superintendent, The Board of Public Instruction of Dade County, Miami, Florida

PAUL M. HALVERSON, School of Education, Syracuse University, Syracuse, New York

HAMILTON, DE FOREST, Superintendent, Sonoma County Schools, California

L. W. HEDGE, Principal, Bakersfield High School, Bakersfield, California

MARION E. HERRIOT, Principal, Airport Junior High School, Los Angeles, California

LEON C. HOOD, Administrative Assistant, Guidance and Placement, Clifford J. Scott High School, East Orange, New Jersey

ROBERT E. JENKINS, Superintendent of Schools, Ridgewood, New Jersey

DONOVAN JOHNSON, Associate Professor of Education, University of Minnesota High School, Minneapolis

COLLEEN KARAVITES, Social Studies Department, Evanston Township High School, Evanston, Illinois

DONALD E. KITCH, Chief, Supplemental Education Services, California State Department of Education, Sacramento

C. DARL LONG, Principal, White Plains High School, New York

DOROTHY McCUSKEY, Professor of Education, Bowling Green State University, Bowling Green, Ohio

JOSEPH C. McLAIN, Principal, Mamaroneck High School, New York

L. S. MICHAEL, Superintendent, Evanston Township High School, Evanston, Illinois

PAUL M. MITCHUM, Assistant Superintendent of Schools, Wilmington, Delaware

JEANNE ORR, Assistant Professor, The University School, Ohio State University, Columbus

JOHN OTTS, Assistant Superintendent, Charlotte City Schools, North Carolina

6

OVID F. PARODY, *Principal, Battle Hill School, White Plains, New York*

DONALD ROE, *Assistant Superintendent of Schools, Gary, Indiana*

OSCAR F. SCHAAF, *Head, Mathematics Department, Eugene High School, Eugene, Oregon*

PAUL SCHWEITZER, *The Bronx High School of Science, New York City*

MARION C. SHERIDAN, *Head, English Department, James Hillhouse High School, New Haven, Connecticut*

ALFRED H. SKOGSBERG, *Principal, Bloomfield Junior High School, Bloomfield, New Jersey*

MARY NEEL SMITH, *Principal, Twenty-Fourth Street School, Denver, Colorado*

EDITH E. STARRATT, *Editor, The Citizenship Journal, Sherburne High School, Sherburne, New York*

ELSWORTH TOMPKINS, *Assistant Secretary, National Association of Secondary School Principals, Washington*

GLENN F. VARNER, *Assistant Superintendent, Secondary and Vocational Education, St. Paul Public Schools, Minnesota*

KIRBY P. WALKER, *Superintendent of Schools, Jackson Public Schools, Jackson, Mississippi*

RAYMOND G. WILSON, *Executive Secretary, Commission on Secondary Schools, Southern Association of Colleges and Secondary Schools, Atlanta, Georgia*

WILFORD H. WOODY, *Principal, West Senior High School, Denver, Colorado*

ROSALIND M. ZAPF, *Denby High School, Detroit, Michigan*

7

ACKNOWLEDGMENTS

The Educational Testing Service, Russell Sage Foundation, and the Executive Editor express their deep indebtedness to the members of the three committees who helped to develop this study and to all other participants in it. In addition, the Executive Editor wants to record his personal thanks to President Henry Chauncey of the Educational Testing Service, to Richard H. Sullivan, its Executive Vice-President at the time the study began, and to many others of its staff who have made themselves available for advice and counsel.

A special word of appreciation is due Robert Dickenson who as executive assistant to the editor not only took care of all the administrative details of the project, but also made valuable editorial suggestions and was entirely responsible for assembling and arranging the materials for the supplementary volume now in preparation, in which appear the original contributions of each of the consultants and reviewers.

The editor also expresses his special appreciation of the insight and understanding administration of the project provided by the Educational Testing Service through the work of John E. Dobbin, Director of the Cooperative Test Division, who served as project director, and to Ann Z. Smith, his assistant, for helpful assistance in carrying the project through to its conclusion and for their critical reading of the manuscript prior to its submission to Russell Sage Foundation for publication. Thanks are also due Margaret R. Dunne of the Foundation staff for her competent and painstaking editorial work on the manuscript.

CONTENTS

TABLES AND CHARTS

9

Education does not mean teaching people to know what they do not know. It means teaching them to behave as they do not behave. . . . It is not teaching the youth of England the shapes of letters and the tricks of numbers; and then leaving them to turn their arithmetic to roguery, and their literature to lust. It is, on the contrary, training them into the perfect exercise and kingly continence of their bodies and souls.

JOHN RUSKIN

FOREWORD

The changes that have characterized the American secondary school in the past fifty years have been a part of the vast changes sweeping through our national life. In this epoch our culture, our economy, and our place in world affairs have undergone transformations so complete as to make them almost revolutionary. Our high schools, too, have changed from rather narrowly defined college preparatory institutions, serving fewer than one in ten young people, to broadly described schools that enroll nearly seven in ten Americans of high school age.

Changes as important and as rapid as those of this twentieth century in the high school naturally produce some lags in public understanding. It is within the memory of living Americans that our high schools were devoted almost wholly to the academic preparation of a few of our young people for college. Since whatever has been done in the past quite automatically becomes "traditional," some of the functions now performed by secondary schools are not fully understood or enthusiastically endorsed by all citizens. In fact, the role of the high school in our modern society has been the subject of warm discussion in many communities. Some interested citizens earnestly contend that the schools should limit their efforts quite strictly to academic instruction. Others, equally concerned and certainly as earnest, support an expansion of school goals to include instruction in a variety of nonacademic fields.

Because the public schools are both created and supported by local communities, public discussions of what the high schools should accomplish are healthful expressions of democracy and usually beneficial to education. Professional educators find it easier to respond to the public will when that will is fully expressed by a community that is paying attention—as well as taxes—to its schools.

11

Discussions of the functions of the high school, however, sometimes divide interested citizens into groups that do not completely understand one another. Some speak of "emphasis on the fundamentals" or "thorough preparation for college"—and have in mind many of the same things as those who speak of "education for life" or "life adjustment." The various names given to general concepts in educational thought tend to become mutually exclusive shibboleths, even though the concepts they describe may overlap in a very large measure. Educators and laymen alike seem unable to express their hopes for education in terms that have precise meaning for all other interested persons. So discussions of what high schools should accomplish have been characterized occasionally by misunderstanding. While public discussion of the goals of education is necessary and good, discussion that produces factionalism and divisive pressures upon the schools only does harm.

Schoolmen and interested citizens are not the only people who have a stake in appropriate description of the goals of secondary schools. Those agencies which serve education—in research, in publishing, in testmaking, in training of teachers, and in other ways—also must design their work according to the expectations held for public education. When expectations appear to run in several directions and are expressed in conflicting or obscure terminology, the specialists who serve the educators become confused too.

Several years ago an organized attempt was made to state in common and useful terms the recognized objectives of American elementary schools. Upon that occasion, Russell Sage Foundation and the Educational Testing Service were joined by the United States Office of Education and the Department of Elementary School Principals of the National Education Association. They jointly sponsored a survey to develop a comprehensive statement of the goals of elementary school education in terms of observable behavior. The report of that study was published by the Foundation in book form under the title *Elementary School Objectives*. The report proved to be useful to citizens and educators concerned with the elementary school. So the National Association of Secondary School Principals proposed that a similar survey study of objectives be conducted at the high school level. From that proposal by the NASSP a project developed—and from the project this book.

Any attempt to state in universally useful language the various expectations held for the public high schools needs cooperative action. There are too many interests involved, too many points of view widely held, for a single person or agency to attack the problem alone. Fortunately, the interest of Russell Sage Foundation in the proposal submitted by the secondary school principals' group made possible an extensive survey project in which other interested groups could be invited to take part. As a consequence, a study of secondary school objectives was undertaken with the joint sponsorship of Russell Sage Foundation, the National Association of Secondary School Principals, and the Educational Testing Service—with ETS serving as the agency for management of the project.

Three other educational organizations accepted invitations to nominate members (not official representatives) for the committees that designed the survey and edited the report: the United States Office of Education, the American Association of School Administrators, and the Association for Supervision and Curriculum Development. Thus, the report contained in this volume represents the combined planning of representatives of six national educational agencies plus the distinguished citizens they called upon for help.

Although the planning for the project was done by a small committee, the really creative work in describing and criticizing the goals of secondary education was done by two fairly large groups of educators. Those who wrote the original statement of objectives—the "consultants"—contributed large amounts of their own time to define the research and philosophy upon which they based their own expectations of education, and to express these definitions in the manner chosen for the project. Those who criticized the original statements in the light of practical school circumstances also contributed significantly to the project by helping to keep it close to reality at every turn. To all who contributed, then—the consultants, the critics, the laymen—the planners of the project are deeply indebted for a vast amount of professional effort generously and willingly given.

The sponsors of the project were extremely fortunate in being able to secure the services of Dr. Will French at the point of his retirement from Teachers' College, Columbia University, after a distinguished career in school administration and college teaching. Dr. French brought to the project as executive editor an experienced mind capable of organizing and editing the creative work of nearly one hundred authors and critics. Much of the usefulness of the report to educators and citizens will be attributable to his insight and wisdom.

This report is *not* a prescription for what any high school should teach or accomplish. It is simply an organized consensus of the expectations that citizens and educators hold for the American high school. The common idiom is that of behavior: What should the student be able and willing to *do*, in an observable way, as a consequence of his high school education? If the report is to have value, that value will come through its use as a common reference by local groups of educators and citizens as they work together in deciding upon the goals of *their* schools in *their* communities.

HENRY CHAUNCEY, *President,*
Educational Testing Service

Princeton, New Jersey
June, 1957

PREFACE

The Survey Study of Behavioral Outcomes of General Education in High School was organized to describe for educators, curriculum planners, testmakers, and interested citizens the objectives of general education in American secondary schools. Other groups and individuals have specified certain general goals that schools seek, or have described the subject matter and learning activities of the high schools. However, no comprehensive and authoritative statement of the *behavioral* goals, or outcomes, of general education in secondary schools has been made. The idea of stating the goals of general education in terms of behavior has been frequently voiced and in *A Design for General Education*[1] general behavioral areas were defined, although the principal kinds of behavior sought within each area were not indicated. Most of the literature on this aspect of general education relates to college students and not to the younger, less mature, and unselected groups of adolescents of high school age. Until now, no attempt has been made to discover and publish a statement of the general consensus of what high school graduates should be able to do—how they may be expected to think and feel and act—as a result of the general education element of their high school program.

Early in 1951 three national educational agencies joined the Educational Testing Service in a survey of the behavioral outcomes of elementary education. This study was made possible by the cooperation of Russell Sage Foundation. The recommendations of a committee composed of some of the country's most distinguished educators were reviewed by critics and teachers and published by the Foundation under the title *Elementary School Objectives:* A Report Prepared for the Mid-Century Committee

[1] McConnell, Thomas R., editor, *A Design for General Education*. American Council on Education, Washington, 1944.

15

on Outcomes in Elementary Education.[1] This report, describing the goals of elementary education in terms of observable behavior, found immediate and wide acceptance and varied uses. Curriculum planners use it as a guide in the selection of learning activities that encourage the development of specific skills at various stages of growth. Parent-teacher groups use it as source material through which home and school may achieve a mutual understanding of children's needs that may be related to school programs and procedures. Citizens and educators use it as a pool of information as they seek a common and clear understanding of the educational goals for particular schools and communities. Educational researchers and test-builders use it to locate those aspects of school growth most in need of further research. This elementary school study continues to affect an increasing number of elementary school programs as it becomes more widely known among educators.

Shortly after the publication of *Elementary School Objectives*, educational leaders at the secondary school level began to inquire about the possibility of a similar study of objectives of general education in high schools. These inquiries led to further discussions until in 1954 the Executive Committee of the National Association of Secondary School Principals of the National Education Association endorsed a proposal by the Educational Testing Service for such a study. The cooperation and support of Russell Sage Foundation transformed this proposal into a project. Advisory aid offered by the United States Office of Education, the American Association of School Administrators, and the Association for Supervision and Curriculum Development accounted for a final decision by the Educational Testing Service to launch the project.

Organization of the Study

Although preliminary planning work had been carried out in part by the Educational Testing Service, Russell Sage Foundation, and a small group of informal representatives of the Na-

---

[1] Kearney, Nolan C., *Elementary School Objectives*. Russell Sage Foundation, New York, 1953.

tional Association of Secondary School Principals,[1] the first steps in formally outlining the scope and method of the study were taken by a Planning and Editorial Committee, convened soon after the project was launched. As can be seen by referring to page 5, this Planning Committee was composed of representatives from each of the sponsoring and advisory agencies plus the executive editor and the administrator serving as project director for the Educational Testing Service. This committee reviewed the preliminary plans for the project, suggested some modifications which were adopted, and served later as an editorial committee that read and criticized a draft of the proposed report before it was submitted to the Foundation.

The work of the committees associated with this project and of the executive editor was aimed at developing and putting into useful form a statement of the principal behavioral outcomes of that part of secondary schooling which is devoted to the general education of all youth. To assist in developing such a statement three working committees were appointed.[2]

1. **Committee of Consultants.** This committee was responsible for developing lists of behavioral outcomes which appear in this report in consolidated and synthesized form as Part III. This committee met once to develop common methods of work and to confer briefly with the Committee of Advisers. Thereafter the consultants worked separately, developing lists of behavioral outcomes and "developmental equivalents" under each of three areas of living in which they considered it important for all youth to be willing and able to behave appropriately and competently. These three behavioral areas will be discussed at length at a later point in this report.

2. **Committee of Advisers.** This committee was composed of interested citizens, the "consumers" of the school's products. It was charged with the task of advising the consultants and reviewing their work in the light of public needs. This committee met

[1] C. Darl Long, Principal, White Plains High School, White Plains, N. Y.; Joseph C. McLain, Principal, Mamaroneck High School, Mamaroneck, N. Y.; Morris Meister, Principal, The Bronx High School of Science, New York City; and Howard G. Spalding, Principal, A. B. Davis High School, Mount Vernon, N. Y.

[2] The membership of these committees is given on pages 5–7.

once with the consultants to discuss their views of public needs affecting secondary education. Although some of the members of this group have special interests in education, they were responsible for presenting all major facets of public concern and with relating their particular interests to the broader interests of the general public. They presented these views to the consultants in a short meeting before the consultants began to develop their lists of proposed behaviors. After the consultants had formulated their recommendations, the advisers worked individually in reviewing and criticizing them.

3. **Committee of Reviewers.** This committee was composed of teachers, administrators, psychologists, and curriculum specialists who are especially familiar with the work of young people in high school. This committee did not meet as a group, but served as individual critics of the behavioral outcomes proposed by the consultants. They examined, evaluated, and commented upon these proposals in the light of their special knowledge about young people and the practicalities of the school situation. Where they felt important behaviors had been omitted, they added suggestions. The final list of behaviors consists of the proposals which were regarded as important by at least three-fourths of the reviewers who evaluated them.

The executive editor was responsible for organizing and synthesizing the work of these various committees, for grouping the suggestions into appropriate clusters of behaviors under suitable headings, and for casting the suggested outcomes into a common pattern for publication. The manuscript was submitted to the members of the Planning and Editorial Committee for criticism and was revised in the light of their suggestions. It was also reviewed by representatives of the Educational Testing Service and Russell Sage Foundation. The report, therefore, does not represent the personal whims and biases of the editor, although on the whole it represents a point of view and a proposal which he is glad to have helped formulate. As printed here, the report is not a personal production, but a general consensus of a large group of persons who are active in, and concerned about, American secondary education. That the consensus was not unanimous among the consultants and reviewers hardly needs to be stated. The proof that they represented various points of view in secondary education is that they did not all always agree upon the emphasis that should be placed upon behaviors in secondary education, upon the ways in which some were stated or upon those which should be included or excluded. Those behaviors now in the lists do, however, represent those upon which there was consensus. In order that each consultant and reviewer might have an opportunity to have his work and views presented, a separate supplementary volume containing the contributions as they were submitted is now in preparation.

WILL FRENCH

Princeton, New Jersey
May, 1957

Part I

GENERAL EDUCATION IN HIGH SCHOOL

In 1918 when Alexander Inglis wrote *Principles of Secondary Education*,[1] he argued that if we were to create enough social cohesiveness in the descendants of peoples drawn from all over the world to remain a nation united in anything but name, we needed to develop an effective program of "integrating" education in the high schools. His recognition of our need for this common program of education led him to maintain that all youth should go to high school so that its benefits would be felt universally. He was among the first of the leaders in the distinctive field of secondary education to sense the social significance of the secondary school, to recognize the secondary school as part of our "common schools," and to stress an "integrating" element in its educational program. All through the first half of the twentieth century other leaders in secondary education have been pointing out the rising need for improvements in the required, "integrating," "common learning," "general education" element in the high school curriculum.[2]

The Cardinal Principles of Secondary Education,[3] also published in 1918, stated for the first time the purposes of education in terms of the societal needs to be served by a secondary education that was being increasingly recognized as an upward extension of the common school's program. Previous committee reports dealing with the secondary school's program had stated its purposes and

---

[1] Inglis, Alexander, *Principles of Secondary Education*. Houghton Mifflin Co., Boston, 1918. Reprinted in 1953.

[2] Association for Supervision and Curriculum Development, *What Shall the High Schools Teach?* National Education Association, Washington, 1956, chap. 5.

[3] Commission on the Reorganization of Secondary Education, *The Cardinal Principles of Secondary Education*. Bureau of Education, Government Printing Office, Washington, 1918.

objectives in terms of the degree of mastery of certain subject-fields which the school was expected to require of its students. If this country needed to have a common integrating program of education in high school as Inglis held, and if the "cardinal principles" of secondary education are those advocated by the Commission on the Reorganization of Secondary Education, then, the existing program of required subjects would have to accomplish these purposes or give place to a program that did. The logic of this was recognized at the time, for soon after the appearance of "the cardinal principles" a whole series of subject-field reports appeared, each professing to show how its subject could achieve one or more of its stated objectives.

Throughout the intervening years the purposes of secondary education as stated by the Commission have been affirmed and reaffirmed in complementary statements by various professional and lay groups, until now there is almost unanimous acceptance of such purposes as basic in determining what the high school curriculum should be. During these years the chief problem has been to decide upon the most effective means of achieving these purposes. The proponents of the conventional group of required subjects have "motivated," "modified," and "enriched" their offerings under pressure but have held closely to the pattern of subjects which was, and still is, the prevailing pattern for the required element in the high school program.[1]

Rising Demand for Curricular Change

The continuing argument for change in the high school's required curriculum to provide for more direct emphasis on the stated purposes grew out of changing conditions in American life which made it apparent that the high school should contribute more positively to the social, civic, and personal effectiveness of all American youth. The costs of poor health and physical disability were recognized in industry and in war mobilization. Increasing instability in home-life in the nation created a demand for better preparation for family responsibilities. The growing

[1] Fieldstra, Clarence, "General Education Courses Required in Los Angeles City and County High Schools," *California Journal of Secondary Education*, vol. 29, May, 1954, pp. 256–262.

complexity of social and civic problems upon which ordinary citizens were asked to pass judgment called for higher levels of ability to make intelligent and informed decisions. The economic problems faced by individuals in their own personal life, as workers and as citizens, made such levels of economic competence as had been attained by youth inadequate to their need. These factors, together with a growing tendency on the part of the public to expect the school to assume a larger share of the responsibility for the growth and development of children and youth, have led to rising demands that the high school modify its program to provide for all young people many kinds of instruction not encompassed by its old required program, and that it focus its central required element on the achievement of the generally accepted purposes of secondary education.

In summing up the findings of The Regents' Inquiry dealing with the high school curriculum, Spaulding voiced the opinion that the socially motivated objectives endorsed in the cardinal principles statement were not being effectively sought by saying:

> The most serious problems are to be found in the lack of tangible connection between what the boys and girls learn while they are in school and what they will need to know after they leave school. A fund of largely academic information, a set of social attitudes picked up at random, tastes and interests developed as chance may dictate, provide no stable basis for the welfare either of individuals or of the State to which they belong. If it is to deserve public support, the program of secondary education must produce more tangible results than at present in the form of systematic preparation for citizenship and leisure and jobs.[1]

The movement in education toward a program which directly undertakes to enable all youth to meet life's needs has come to be known as the "general education" movement. Its adherents accept the stated purposes of secondary education as paramount ends in the education of all youth and are willing to abandon preconceived notions of how this program should be organized in favor of any plan that gives promise of being an effective means toward these ends. Recently there has also been much discussion

[1] Reprinted by permission from *High School and Life*, by Francis T. Spaulding. Copyright, 1939. McGraw-Hill Book Co., New York, p. 120.

of the purposes and functions of a required integrating program of education for college freshmen and sophomores and of how to achieve it. One of the results has been the development of several new types of required college programs to which the term "general education" has been applied. Each of these programs is claimed by its proponents to afford a good way of achieving the purposes of a common, required element in an educational program. Because these lower division college programs and those of high schools share the same basic purposes, a renewed concern over the required high school program has been in part a result of college level innovations.[1] As far back as 1893 the Committee of Ten used the term and held that general education in the high school consisted of four major subjects: language, science, history, and mathematics. That the required high school program still tends to be considered a program of general education—whether good or bad—is shown by an increasing use of the term in connection with secondary education. An example of this is the publication of *General Education in the American High School* by the North Central Association of Colleges and Secondary Schools.[2] The listings of articles in the *Education Index* also show how commonly and increasingly the term is now being applied to secondary education. The major question to be faced, then, is not whether general education *should* be a part of the high school curriculum, but rather how we can develop the *most effective* high school program of general education.

FOUR BASIC QUESTIONS

An effort to solve this problem requires that we address ourselves to four basic questions.

1. What are the purposes to be accomplished in high school by a program of general education?

Granted that we have generally accepted objectives for secondary education, what basic purposes are to be served *for all youth* by the general education element in the program?

[1] For example, *General Education in School and College:* A Committee Report by Members of the Faculties of Andover, Exeter, Lawrenceville, Harvard, Princeton, and Yale. Harvard University Press, Cambridge, 1952.

[2] Corey, Stephen M., and others, *General Education in the American High School.* Scott, Foresman and Co., New York, 1942.

2. What is the nature of the desired outcomes of a really effective program of general education in high school?
What shall teachers look for and accept as a realization of the purposes of general education?

3. What are the best proofs of the success of general education in high school?
What evidence can be accepted as constituting some proof of success of efforts at general education?

4. How broad a scope is general education in high school to have?
What defensible limits can be set for what, under any circumstances, must be a broad program?

If we are to take a new look at this element of the high school's program, it would seem that such questions must be answered before there can be wise choices as to content and methods of instruction. The first requisite is that we set aside preconceived notions of what this program should consist of; that we relinquish, at least temporarily, any prior commitments to particular subjects or ways of organizing the program; that we set goals important enough to command our full allegiance; and that we be willing to use those means for their attainment which our intelligence, professional research, and educational philosophy support.

The Question of Purpose

Perhaps the best approach to this first question can be made if we refer to some of the statements of purpose developed by those who have given general education the most serious study. The following extract is from an article on General Education prepared by T. R. McConnell and others for the *Encyclopedia of Educational Research.*

> The purpose of general education is to enable men and women to live rich and satisfying lives and to undertake the responsibilities of citizenship in a free society. Although general education seeks to discover and nurture individual talent, it emphasizes preparation for activities in which men engage in common as citizens, workers, and members of family and community groups.

Thus conceived, general education is not sharply distinguished from liberal education; the two differ mainly in degree, not in kind. General education undertakes to redefine liberal education in terms of life's problems as men face them, to give it human orientation and social direction, to invest it with content that is directly relevant to the demands of contemporary society. General education is liberal education with its matter and method shifted from its original aristocratic intent to the service of democracy. General education seeks to extend to all men the benefits of an education that liberates.[1]

McConnell and others writing earlier in *A Design for General Education* said:

For the purposes of this report, general education refers to those phases of non-specialized, non-vocational education that should be the common possession, the common denominator, so to speak, of educated persons as individuals and as citizens in a free society. . . .[2]

B. Lamar Johnson describes general education as "the part of education which is concerned with the common knowledge, skills and attitudes needed by each individual to be effective as a person, a member of a family, a worker and a citizen. . . ."[3]

In an article entitled "Fundamental Issues in General Education" in the *Journal of General Education*, Ralph W. McDonald says of objectives:

The goals of the general education program must be realistic. They must be conceived in terms of the behavior of the individual student. They must focus clearly upon the attitudes, capacities, abilities, and values which are expected to be built into the lives of the students. Furthermore, the goals must point directly to the elements in the heritage of free, Western, democratic society which are considered to be the common possession of college-trained people. . . . The ultimate test of the success of all general education can be had only in the evidences of constructive living on the part of those who have been reached by the program. . . .[4]

---

[1] McConnell, T. R., and others, "General Education," *Encyclopedia of Educational Research*, edited by Walter S. Monroe. Macmillan Co., New York, 1950, p. 489.

[2] McConnell, T. R., editor, *A Design for General Education*. American Council on Education, Washington, 1944.

[3] Johnson, B. Lamar, *General Education in Action*. American Council on Education, Washington, 1952, p. 20.

[4] McDonald, Ralph W., "Fundamental Issues in General Education," *Journal of General Education*, October, 1949, pp. 34, 38.

Further evidence of general agreement on the purposes of general education is furnished by Dressel and Mayhew:

> . . . There is less disagreement about general education objectives than about the means of achieving them. . . . The objectives found in *A Design for General Education, General Education in Action,* and the *Report of the President's Commission* [*on Higher Education in American Democracy*] are illustrative of the better and most commonly accepted statements.[1]

Underlying these statements are two correlated purposes for general education: one concerned with the person as an individual, the other concerned with him as a citizen. The first proposes that general education help each young person realize his fullest potentialities. It recognizes each youth as a maturing individual who has not yet reached the levels of physical, mental, social-civic, economic, or vocational maturity he should reach as a mature adult. It therefore seeks to help youth become all that it is within them to be. It recognizes that self-realization, not self-preservation, is the first law of human life—that human nature seeks to *become* and is not satisfied merely to *be*. It operates on the assumption that human organisms are born with, and soon develop, certain common, basic, primary needs which demand satisfaction. The social matrix into which they are born modifies these and adds other common secondary needs. It is inevitable that, as human organisms living in a dynamic social situation, they will strive so to utilize and develop the capacities which they possess that they are better able to satisfy these needs.

Only when faced with prolonged and complete frustration do human beings cease trying to become something which to them seems better than what they are. Allport in his *Becoming* calls attention to a group of psychologists "who in common postulate one basic motive in life—the maintaining, actualizing and enhancing of the capacities of the individual organism."[2] The first

---

[1] Dressel, Paul L., and Lewis B. Mayhew, *General Education.* American Council on Education, Washington, 1954, p. 2.

[2] Allport, Gordon W., *Becoming: Basic Considerations for a Psychology of Personality.* Yale University Press, New Haven, 1955, p. 16.

27

purpose of general education, therefore, is based upon the proposition that the various common capabilities of young people should be developed as fully as possible through education so that they will be able to utilize them as needed in the planning and the living of their own lives. If human personality is as sacred as we in the western world maintain, then no program of general education which is to be required of all can fail to seek to attain this goal of individual development.

The second of the two coordinated purposes of general education stressed in the foregoing quotations is concerned with the growth of youth toward responsible citizenship. The words "responsible citizens" are used in their broadest sense to include the common relationships one has with other people in face-to-face situations, as well as those arising as one cooperates on a less personal basis in political, social, economic, or cultural organizations. That education in this country should be designed to help all young people become responsible citizens in this sense, is as essential as that it should help each to realize his individual potentialities. The very existence of the democratic state demands it. Without the universally shared willingness and ability of each citizen to act as intelligently as possible upon matters of public concern, democratically oriented societies are bound to fall far short of their declared purposes.

Consequently, important as a democracy conceives human personality to be, the development of individual potentials cannot be the sole aim of a program of general education for its youth. Our society expects that each of these developed personalities will contribute his share to its maintenance and improvement. These personalities cannot be educated for withdrawal from society or for detached, indifferent observation of the social scene. A democratic society cannot afford the luxury of such aloofness on the part of any of its citizens, and certainly not on the part of the most intelligent segment of its educated members. Any educational program required of all by a democratically oriented state must be expected to cultivate the willingness and ability of each member to contribute as best he can to the development of his society. The public's expectation of active, constructive participation from its citizens accounts for the fact that those "ivory tower" intellectuals in this country who seek to influence society by their Jovian thunderbolts of criticism and complaint, exert much less influence than the practicing intellectuals who actually get their hands dirty in the real work of building a better democratic social order. Our country expects its best educated citizens to possess exact and extensive knowledge, but its highest praise goes to them when they show that they have the "know-how" to put this knowledge to work. In our public's view the significance of possessing knowledge lies in its relevance to action. Our people evidently believe with Thomas Henry Huxley that "the great end of life is not knowledge, but action." Or as Whitehead puts it: "Pedants sneer at an education which is useful. But if education is not useful, what is it? Is it talent, to be hidden away in a napkin? Of course, education should be useful, whatever your aim in life."[1]

No modern state is, and probably no past national state ever was, altruistic enough to tolerate and pay for an educational program the main purpose of which is to encourage its youth generally to withdraw from its group life. The United States certainly is in no position today to countenance a program of universal general education, either in public or private schools, which along with its purpose of developing individual capacity to the fullest, is not equally concerned with the creation of both a willingness and an ability to contribute to our society's welfare, even when—one might say especially when—participation in public affairs by well-educated men and women is sometimes disparaged and discouraged. No program of general education can escape making an effective contribution to the civic competence of all youth.

Of interest on this point is what David Schoenbrun has to say in a recent article on "Manners and Morals of the French" in *Harper's Magazine*. Close contact with contemporary French life and institutions gained as Columbia Broadcasting System's representative gives this layman's views particular pertinence.

[1] Reprinted by permission from *The Aims of Education*, and Other Essays, by Alfred North Whitehead. Copyright, 1929. Macmillan Co., New York, p. 14.

29

. . . Of all the institutions, of all the influences upon French life the one I believe to be most responsible for the lack of community spirit that divides the French people and weakens their government is the educational system.

A sense of community with others is not, I suspect, a "natural" human instinct. . . . Man is gregarious—but he is also aggressive and spends most of his time quarreling with the neighbor whose company he seeks.

A community spirit is thus an acquired characteristic. It can only be acquired at a very early age. Once a man is full grown it is probably too late to make him public-spirited and civic-minded. This is precisely the case of Frenchmen. The French educational system does not attempt to develop a sense of civic pride or community spirit in the child. It is keyed to the development of the individual. Its most iniquitous feature, however, is its refusal to allow for individual differences in capacity. Where the American system aims at helping each child attain his own maximum capacity, the French system is based upon individual achievement through competition. The French child is measured not only by his mastery of the subject matter, but above all in relation to all other children. It is child against child in competitive examinations.

This is a cruel system. The bright children become intellectual snobs, proudly wearing the proof of their superiority. The less bright, the average child, is humiliated and frequently crushed by a feeling of inadequacy. This constant competition, this harping on distinction or disgrace, can only result in the bitter rivalry, jealousies, and discord which I find to be characteristic of French society.

It is in the area of education for citizenship that the French system is most dangerously negligent. It is no surprise to see that French politics are always in crisis. . . . Politicians blame it upon a faulty constitution. I would put part of the blame on the schools. . . . The best constitution is useless when administered by disorderly, uncooperative individuals, which is what most of France's legislators are. They may be educated, literate men. Their brilliance, however, is lost in the spiritual wasteland of the French community, to a great extent because they never acquired the sense of community in the jungle of the competitive school system.[1]

We have said that the two purposes of individual development and active citizenship are correlated, but actually may they not be two aspects of the *same* purpose? The fulfillment of either one

[1] Schoenbrun, David, "Manners and Morals of the French," *Harper's Magazine*, March, 1957, pp. 54–55.

rests upon fulfillment of the other. This seems to touch on the old question of whether the organization of society tends to enslave or to liberate the individuals who constitute it. Only in a democratic social order does this apparent antagonism tend to resolve itself. While it is true that the democratic state tolerates private education and supports public education as it tends "to preserve itself and to promote its own best interest," yet the democratic state does this as a means of serving the basic purpose of its existence. The democratically oriented state, unlike other forms of societal organization, has a purpose and function beyond and outside itself; it has a prior commitment to the continuous safeguarding and cultivation of the full development of all the individuals who compose that state. The most legitimate reason for its wanting to preserve itself is that it may perform this function for its citizens. It supports education as an important means of performing this function. Only in a democracy do the ends sought by the society from education and the concern of each person for full growth and development tend to coincide. Only in a democracy is it so evident that if one throws himself freely into the affairs of his time, he does not thereby lose his opportunity for his own full and free development—but gains it for himself and others. So these two correlated purposes of any program of general education for all youth in the United States can be said to merge almost into one purpose. This fact accounts for the presence and importance of a required, "integrating" program of "general education" in our high schools. It makes the evaluation and improvement of the existing general education program in each high school the most important responsibility of its professional staff.

The Nature of Outcomes

Wide agreement on the purposes of general education leads us naturally into a consideration of the second pertinent question, which deals with the nature of the desired outcomes of general education in high school. These outcomes are achieved in high school as the required general education program tends to produce young men and women who not only acquire knowledge of, but are willing and able to apply in their daily lives, our moral, ethical, and spiritual standards; to sense our cultural and social values; and to use the generalizations and principles of the social and physical sciences. Knowledge of our culture's evolving and developing ideals, standards, values, and technology is not enough. Our young people must be eager and able to convert these "things of the spirit" into the flesh and blood of personal and group living before the purposes of general education are realized. General education must transform these abstract intangibles into the concrete realities of behavior before we can be sure that it has achieved its intended purposes.

Although current curricular practice does not generally provide explicit statements of the behavioral outcomes of general education, acceptance of outcomes stated in terms of behavior is reflected in the writing of many who have given the problem the most thought. A few quotations will illustrate the point. The following statement is quoted from the previously mentioned article in the *Encyclopedia of Educational Research*.

> The purposes of general education are better understood in terms of performance or behavior rather than more narrowly in terms of knowledge.[1]

Again in *A Design for General Education* the authors state:

> The committee's second step was to agree upon the broad areas that should be included in general education. These fundamental elements were expressed, not as fields of knowledge, but as the ways in which educated men might properly be expected to behave. The outcomes in other words are defined in terms of performance. General Education, for example, should lead the student to improve and maintain his own health and take his share of responsibility for protecting the health of others; to do his part as an active and intelligent citizen in dealing with the interrelated social, economic and political problems of American life and in solving the problems of post-war international reconstruction; to choose a vocation that will make optimum use of his talents and enable him to make an appropriate contribution to the needs of society.[2]

Leonard, in the *Proceedings* of the 1951 National Conference on Higher Education, expresses the belief that:

[1] McConnell, T. R., *op. cit.*, p. 490.
[2] McConnell, T. R., *op. cit.*, p. 8.

The objectives of general education are based upon the needs of society and of youth in a given time and place. If the goal of America is to provide an environment where freedom can flourish, then the function of general education is to develop free men who will design a society conducive to this philosophy.[1]

Spaulding's comment on the high school curriculum in general is:

Analysis of the present high school curriculum has made evident one paramount reason for a lack of social competence among young people just out of high school. That reason consists in the schools' failure to give boys and girls a chance to acquire many of the abilities and attitudes which the out-of-school world will almost certainly demand of them. In any better program of secondary education a prime essential must therefore be a curriculum more directly focused on the kinds of competence which young people out of school will surely need.[2]

The Fifty-First Yearbook of the National Society for the Study of Education, *General Education*, includes the following quotation:

President Conant states that he would amend the Harvard report on *General Education in Free Society* ". . . by stressing the type of *behavior* on which a free society depends rather than emphasizing the common knowledge and common values which influence the behavior of citizens."[3]

These statements were made when general education in college was being considered, but it would seem reasonable to assume that they apply with equal force to the secondary school level. They seem to indicate a general acceptance of the idea that behavioral competence is the best way to describe the legitimate outcomes of general education. The most convincing evidence that increased social competence is being achieved is the kind and quality of behavior which youth are being encouraged to learn in school and which young adults who are graduates of high school exhibit in life situations. Behavior is the most reliable index

---

[1] National Conference on Higher Education, *Proceedings*. National Education Association, Washington, 1951, p. 173.

[2] Spaulding, Francis T., *op. cit.*, p. 261.

[3] National Society for the Study of Education, *General Education:* Fifty-First Yearbook, Part I. University of Chicago Press, Chicago, 1952, p. 6. (Italics, mine. EDITOR).

we have both of self-realization and of ability to live the responsible life of a citizen in a free society. A program of general education designed primarily to achieve any other kinds of outcomes, even though they may be indirectly related to behavioral willingness and competence, too often results in the acceptance of these means as ends in themselves and of assumed capacity to behave as a valid substitute for actual behavior. The evaluation of a program of general education in terms of anything but behavioral competence substitutes an indirect, and perhaps an unreliable and inappropriate, measure for one that is direct and pertinent. Two of the first steps toward further improvement in the high school's general education program would seem to be: (1) the acceptance of the idea that its outcomes are best described in terms of behavioral competence, and (2) the development of more explicit statements of some of the principal kinds and levels of behavior which it is reasonable for general education in high school to undertake to achieve.

What Are the Best Proofs of the Success of a General Education Program?

The third basic question asks how we may be more certain that the overall behavioral objectives of general education in high school are being achieved. It is clear from a study of the literature devoted to the high school curriculum that the mere statement of a *general* objective is not considered an adequate definition of the goals of a high school program. Many authors have expanded their statements of general objectives with statements of implied "specific" objectives. Generally, however, these do not supply specific behavioral outcomes. The McConnell Committee in *A Design for General Education*, as we have shown, recognized the need for stating outcomes in terms of what is called in its report "performance." This committee, therefore, listed as "elements" the knowledge and understanding, skills, abilities, and attitudes and appreciations thought to be the means of achieving each of its general goals.[1] No doubt this committee had in mind certain

[1] See also Anderson, Vernon E., Paul R. Grim, and William T. Gruhn, *Principles and Practices of Secondary Education.* Ronald Press, New York, 1951, pp. 36–38.

behaviors which it thought would be achieved by one possessing these "elements," but it did not state explicitly what particular kinds of "performance" were to be sought. Many other current statements of the major objectives of general education imply that behavior is the real measure of its success, yet they are not generally as helpful to teachers as they could be, because they have not been specific enough in indicating the kinds and levels of competence which it is reasonable for teachers to strive for. "Good citizenship," for example, is a universally listed and generally accepted objective for elementary and secondary education. But what are some of the principal behaviors which, if manifested by students, would indicate reasonable growth toward important aspects of civic competence? A valid statement illustrative of some of the most important of these behaviors is imperative if the best results are to be attained by many teachers, and it would be helpful even to the best of teachers in the teaching of citizenship in our high schools. This is true also of such objectives as "health" or "economic competence." What are the behaviors to be observed in a junior high school student which indicate growth and development toward competence to maintain and improve his own physical and mental health or to help solve home, school, or community health and safety problems? Or again, what behaviors on the part of a senior high school student would be indicative of his increasing "economic efficiency"? The lack of more definite specifications in such fields permits some teachers to nourish the vain hope that so long as students are required to take courses in the social and biological sciences they will automatically become good citizens and healthy individuals who are economically literate.

Those responsible for this study believe that more specific illustrative statements of the behaviors to be sought are essential if general education programs in high schools are to be effective in achieving their admitted objectives. Selection of content and other experiences will be improved if both students and teachers have a clearer idea of some of the principal specific behaviors which instruction is supposed to facilitate. Statements that go far enough beyond general objectives to provide examples of specific behaviors will give students and teachers the best proof available of whether the outcomes of general education are actually being achieved. Obviously, these proofs are more easily observed where behavior is overt. But not all behavior is overt; therefore, some indirect evidence of competence to behave will be required in judging results. If a student now spells correctly the words he uses more often than he did previously, one has overt evidence of improved competence to behave in situations involving spelling. But how a student's attitudes toward members of another race have been changed by instruction may not be so overtly and directly revealed. This difficulty of testing directly the results of teaching is not one which arises for the first time when behavioral competence is proposed as the outcome of teaching. Its existence probably accounts for the willingness of teachers to accept knowledge of history, for example, as a substitute for evidence of civic competence. This difficulty, however, does not justify the substitution of other and less reliable tests of results. Nor does it justify abandoning efforts to attain a desired outcome. The home, the church, and the school have long met this difficulty by using the best obtainable indirect evidence of goal-attainment. This often consists of observations of behavior that appear to be related to the goal sought. The teacher who accepts changed behavior as the best evidence of the results of his teaching, and who therefore begins to observe students more closely, will discover more indirect evidence of whether students are acquiring new attitudes, feelings, and appreciations than he is likely at first to think possible. The more specific we can be about the behaviors we desire as results of teaching, the more probable it is that we have made it possible for teachers to identify some evidence, either direct or indirect, of behavioral competence in students.

Proposals that the desired outcomes of general education be stated in terms of specific behaviors may lead some to fear that we propose to make secondary education a process of developing automatic, unthinking responses on the part of youth. The tone of what has already been said in this report should quiet any such fears. To remove the last basis for this anxiety, let it be said here explicitly that the school's task is to provide the possibility of experiences which encourage and facilitate individual students in the intelligent adoption of better standards and patterns of behavior than might otherwise be the case. This means that a program of general education should undertake to channel the student's intellectual capacities into the tasks of self-realization and responsible citizenship. Such a program is intellectual in the best sense of the word, because it assumes that students are not only expected to know something but are also expected to know how to use what they know and to have the disposition to do so. Building up in students an increased store of remembered knowledge is not by itself an acceptable objective of general education. Its objectives are attained only when students "know" in the sense that they exhibit intelligence in their use of knowledge. That the word "know" has these two meanings is well illustrated by McClellan in the *Teachers College Record:*

> This [knowing something] may mean, on the one hand, that some persons know certain propositions or statements—roughly in the sense that they can state the proposition, can define the terms of the proposition, perhaps ostensively, and, finally, can offer some reasoning for the belief that the proposition is true. It may mean, on the other hand, that certain *persons exhibit a kind of behavior that might be characterized by efficiency in relating means to ends, by purposeful organization of various phases of an action, and the like.*[1]

Being an intelligent person, then, can be demonstrated by the possession of knowledge or by competence in its use. The importance of a person's possessing certain knowledge is pretty generally gauged in our culture by how it affects his behavior. Obviously, he who uses knowledge effectively must possess it. The question is not, therefore, whether a student should possess knowledge or use it. It is rather whether a program of general education should be "down-graded" because it accepts improved behavior as evidence of a student's intellectual capacity or of his having learned. Whitehead expresses his view in these words:

> The importance of knowledge lies in its use, in our active mastery of it—that is to say, it lies in wisdom. It is a convention to speak of

[1] McClellan, James E., "Knowledge and the Curriculum," *Teachers College Record*, March, 1956, p. 411. (Italics mine, EDITOR)

mere knowledge, apart from wisdom, as of itself imparting a peculiar dignity to its possessor. I do not share in this reverence for knowledge as such. It all depends on who has the knowledge and what he does with it.[1]

One of the basic ethical ideals of our western culture calls for dynamic rather than static intelligence: for doing, not merely being. We are not only educated by doing but we should be educated for doing. As the committee responsible for *General Education in School and College* remarks of the liberally educated man, "But service to his society and his God, not personal satisfaction alone, is the purpose of his excelling."[2] It would appear, then, that a program of general education which effectively seeks behavioral outcomes by encouraging a reasoned choice of behavior is a program of intellectual education in the best sense of the word. It is therefore concluded that the objectives of a general education program ought to be stated in terms of some of the principal kinds of behavior which are to be sought as its outcomes and that, to be effective, it should provide teachers with more clearcut indications of what these behaviors are. It would also seem desirable to provide some illustrations of the suggested levels of behavior that may be expected both of younger and of older adolescents of varying ranges of maturity.

Recognition of the desirability of teachers' being able to plan their work and to evaluate its success in terms of more specific statements of desirable behavioral outcomes than were available to them led Russell Sage Foundation and the Educational Testing Service to develop the project which resulted in the publication in 1953 of *Elementary School Objectives*.[3] That volume provides a well-organized outline of some of the principal outcomes to be sought in the elementary school. The present project continues the task on through the high school period. The project is not intended

[1] Whitehead, Alfred North, *op. cit.*, p. 43.

[2] *General Education in School and College:* A Committee Report by Members of the Faculties of Andover, Exeter, Lawrenceville, Harvard, Princeton, and Yale. Harvard University Press, Cambridge, 1952, p. 20.

[3] Kearney, Nolan C., *Elementary School Objectives.* Russell Sage Foundation, New York, 1953.

to supply endless lists of minute behaviors. A job analysis of all the behaviors involved in achieving the outcomes of general education is not needed even if it were possible to make such lists. But there is a need at the high school level felt in common by these two organizations and the associated advisory associations, for sharper definitions of the principal areas of behavioral competence, and for a listing of specific illustrative behaviors in each area.

The Scope of General Education in High School

This section undertakes to provide an answer to the fourth basic question presented on page 25. It proposes to define and delimit the scope of general education in high school. Any listing of examples of desired behavioral outcomes should be comprehensive enough to cover the common behavioral situations in students' lives in which general education seeks to affect "performance" or behavior. By definition general education seeks to meet the *common* needs of youth for competence as a person and as a citizen. Special education serves, on the other hand, more individual needs growing out of cultural or intellectual interests, personal strengths and shortcomings, or one's specific vocational plans. If teachers of general education subjects in secondary schools are to be helped to focus their work and the interest of their pupils on important commonly needed behavioral outcomes, there must be more definite agreement on the areas of "common" competence to which general education should give attention. Some of these areas of competence are essential principally because they are basic to self-realization in our society. Others are important because they are basic to responsible citizenship. Perhaps all areas contribute, in at least a minor way, to both of these purposes of general education.

The broad scope of these needs has been indicated by many writers with a telling degree of unanimity. The following statement of "goals" taken from a section of the *Report of the President's Commission on Higher Education* entitled "Establishing the Goals" will serve to show how broad and general most of these objectives are:

1. To develop for the regulation of one's personal and civic life a code of behavior based on ethical principles consistent with democratic ideals.

2. To participate actively as an informed and responsible citizen in solving the social, economic, and political problems of one's community, State, and Nation.

3. To recognize the interdependence of the different peoples of the world and one's personal responsibility for fostering international understanding and peace.

4. To understand the common phenomena in one's physical environment, to apply habits of scientific thought to both personal and civic problems, and to appreciate the implications of scientific discoveries for human welfare.

5. To understand the ideas of others and to express one's own effectively.

6. To attain a satisfactory emotional and social adjustment.

7. To maintain and improve his own health and to cooperate actively and intelligently in solving community health problems.

8. To understand and enjoy literature, art, music, and other cultural activities as expressions of personal and social experience, and to participate to some extent in some form of creative activity.

9. To acquire the knowledge and attitudes basic to a satisfying family life.

10. To choose a socially useful and personally satisfying vocation that will permit one to use to the full his particular interests and abilities.

11. To acquire and use the skills and habits involved in critical and constructive thinking.[1]

This statement may seem to imply a scope for general education which is as broad as that of all of education. In one sense this is true, and ought to be true. But general education's task in each of these eleven areas is to seek that growth and development which is needed by all youth. Specialized education continues, both in the secondary and higher schools, the process of self-

[1] *Higher Education for American Democracy.* Harper and Bros., New York, 1947, vol. 1, pp. 50 ff. See also the Statement of Objectives accepted by the Senate of the University of Minnesota and quoted in the *Encyclopedia of Educational Research, loc. cit.*

realization begun in general education by providing more complete and detailed experiences with one or more of these goals for particular students. The problem before us is not that of deciding which of these areas to exclude from general education, but rather that of deciding how far we should go toward each of these goals.

In general, we are in the position of having widely approved general objectives or goals for the high schools' required programs of general education. We also have a wealth of good content which can be used in reaching these goals. But by not having clear ideas of what kinds and levels of behavioral competence we want the content of general education to help youth achieve, we fail to get as good results in their lives and personalities as we desire. We cannot obtain good results from the indiscriminate use of content, no matter how excellent, any more than a physician can draw upon a store of medicines—all good—without knowing what effects he seeks on the patient. Before the wisest use can be made of available materials and experiences, we need to know specifically, and in some detail, what common behavioral competencies high school teachers should be encouraging and facilitating in their general education courses. It would seem that teachers of general education courses, guided by the accepted goals for general education and given some more definite examples of the outcomes to be sought, expressed in terms of the more important kinds of desired behavior, would get a better sense of direction; would be better able to plan their work; and could make better use of existing content and better evaluate the results of their teaching.

The goals stated above were formulated for college programs, but they have much in common if, indeed, they are not identical with those of general education in elementary and high schools. There are, however, some factors to be taken into account which help to define and limit the scope of a program leading to these goals in high school. First, it should be recognized that the achievement of these goals is not considered to be the exclusive responsibility of general education, of high school education, nor even of all education. It is freely admitted that large contributions to their achievement are properly made by nonschool agencies and that this may sharply reduce the responsibility of the school for a particular goal. Some would prefer that the home, church, and other nonschool agencies be entirely responsible for the achievement of *some* of these goals; that they be *more* responsible for the achievement of some of these goals; or that they be *more* responsible for *some* achievement of *all* of them. Seldom are the lines of responsibility sharply enough defined to relieve the school of its obligation in any goal area. Rightly or wrongly, high schools increasingly are expected to bear a major or minor responsibility for facilitating and encouraging the youth of our communities to show by their behavior that they are growing and developing in all of the ways implied by these goals of general education. The relative importance of any one of these goals in the education of all youth and the amount of responsibility to be borne by secondary education may vary with both time and place, but the trend is such that every high school should assume that it has some responsibility for each goal and should attempt to determine the degree of responsibility its community wants it to assume.

Second, youth of junior and senior high school ages present the high schools with a wide range in each of several types of maturity. This means that some concepts inherent in these goals cannot be grasped by some junior and senior high school students because their feelings of need for growth and development are different from those of more mature individuals. Some complex behaviors implied by these goals are beyond the physical, mental, or emotional capacities of some youth of these ages. On the other hand, some details of personal health and basic safety practices, for example, should be a part of the behaviors sought in the elementary and secondary school, although rightly omitted in college. Dressel and Mayhew report that college faculties frequently tend to reject health, family life, and choice of vocation as of *major* concern in the college general education program,[1] although these would generally be accepted as of major concern in high school. Behaviors proposed as outcomes of general education in high school must take into account what it is reasonable to

[1] Dressel, Paul L., and Lewis B. Mayhew, *op. cit.*, pp. 4–7.

expect a high school to accomplish with its students and what is appropriate for young people of these ranges of maturity.

Third, and related to the second, is the unselectedness of junior and senior high school student populations. First- and second-year college students are a more selected group than high school students, and upper-division college students are even more selected. Behavioral outcomes proposed for use in high schools and expected by teachers from students must take into account wider ranges of difference in home backgrounds, economic status of the family, community surroundings, and other factors known to affect and limit or enhance the behavioral capacity of particular individuals than those proposed for colleges.

Fourth, the goals of general education have been developed under the assumption that the overriding purposes of general education are self-realization and responsible citizenship. This fact needs to be restated here because it not only gives scope but sets limits to the responsibility of general education. In developing programs of general education in high school, we should look at each goal and ask ourselves what important *common* behaviors could be sought in each area that would be indicative of growth toward self-realization. We should also look at each goal and ask what important *common* behaviors could be sought in each area that would be indicative of growth toward responsible citizenship. Behaviors that cannot be accepted by competent adults as warranting some effort by the high school toward the attainment of self-realization or responsible citizenship by all youth, can be set aside as beyond the scope of the principal behaviors general education in high school should seek. General education should leave to special education those levels and kinds of competence that lie outside the common ones attainable, at least at a minimum level, by all youth.

This vital step of supporting these purposes and goals with more detailed statements of behavioral outcomes, toward which some progress may be reasonably sought by general education teachers in the junior and senior high schools, has been heretofore too largely left to chance. As Superintendent Archibald B. Shaw says in an article entitled "The Random Falls Idea":

One whole set of questions urgently needs answers not yet available. This set is illustrated by taking a general goal or objective, breaking it down into sub-goals, and then setting out an ascending series of measurable stages of development building towards that sub-goal.

If, for instance, one of the goals is "the ability [of each youth] to think critically, to express himself clearly and to exercise his own judgment as a responsible citizen," and one were to take as a sub-goal the exercise of judgment as a responsible citizen, just what could be expected of a 14-year old, a 15-year old, a 16-year old who is successfully working towards that goal? The mere posing of the question is difficult. Yet literally thousands such must be answered sometime, somewhere.[1]

The School's Responsibility for Youth's Behavioral Choices

This study has assumed from its inception that the high school should be an active, responsible social agency helping youth to develop common kinds and levels of behaviors in all aspects of living, competence in which is essential if students are to capitalize their own personal resources and to continue to do so independently in their post-high school or college life. Any failure on the part of the high school today to concentrate in general education on the common important behaviors involved in self-realization shortchanges many students. This study assumes also that the high school ought to stress the development of levels of behaviors involved in the discharge of the obligations of responsible citizens in a free society. It is up to secondary education, as the top level of required universal education in our society, to be sure that its students become as competent to think, feel, and act —to behave—as citizens as it is possible for school education to help them to be. Any failure on the part of the high school today to concentrate in general education on the behavioral competencies which are the earmarks of the responsible citizen shortchanges America and the world, for it does not produce as independently minded, competent, responsible citizens as it could.

Today many agencies and organizations are seeking to influence and control the minds and behaviors of men. The powers of

[1] Shaw, Archibald B., and John Lyon Reid, "The Random Falls Idea," *The School Executive*, March, 1956, p. 86.

mass communication are being utilized to serve the bad, the ugly, and the false as well as the good, the beautiful, and the true. Only young people who have acquired desirable patterns of thought and action, and who know why they are desirable and are skillful in sound ways of modifying them or developing new ones, are safe in the world today. And the world is not safe without such young people. The school fails if it does not do its best to produce young people with these competencies. Relative to the importance and possibility of exercising increased control over human behavior, the noted University of Chicago psychologist, Carl R. Rogers, recently remarked:

> What I have been trying to say is that the growing body of knowledge in the behavioral sciences gives to our modern culture an astonishing power of choice. We know how to influence and mold behavior and personality in a great many significant ways. We also have available the choice of whether to set the conditions which develop a suggestible, submissive, unsure individual who can be easily influenced to behave in any way that "we" think wise, or the conditions which will develop an open, adaptive, independent, free-thinking, self-respecting individual. It is this latter person who will perhaps be able to use with intelligence and sensitivity to human values the enormous powers which the physical and behavioral sciences are putting at his disposal. The issue of what choice to make in this regard constitutes, I believe, the challenge of tomorrow both for education and for our whole culture.[1]

That good teachers are in agreement as to which of these two types of individuals they want their work to develop is reflected in the almost universal acceptance of the general objectives of education. There is a question, however, often raised by laymen, as well as by members of the profession, as to the effectiveness of the present required programs of general education in high school in helping each boy and girl to grow and develop toward becoming an "open, adaptive, independent, free-thinking, self-respecting individual." We need to have a better understanding of what kinds of educative experience help to develop the willing-

[1] Rogers, Carl R., "Implications of Recent Advances in Prediction and Control of Behavior," *Teachers College Record*, February, 1956, pp. 320–321.

ness and ability to sustain the kinds and levels of behaviors, and hence help to create the kinds of personality that mark such individuals. We can then proceed more intelligently to evaluate what we are now doing in general education in high school and to make with more certainty the kinds of changes in it that we discover to be necessary.

Part II

CAPITALIZING THE RESULTS OF
THIS STUDY

Part I has stated that the purpose of this study is to develop lists of behavioral outcomes, or goals, of general education in high school and has shown why such lists would be helpful to high schools in the further improvement of their programs of general education. This section proposes to suggest more specifically how the results of this study might be used by various persons who have an interest in, or a responsibility for, a high school's general education program. Classroom teachers, members of curriculum committees, curriculum coordinators, principals, superintendents, members of state departments of education, college teachers, or members of lay committees are likely to have somewhat different responsibilities for general education, and the uses which they might make of the results of this study will vary accordingly.

It seemed to the staff of this project that study of these lists would be facilitated if some of their possible uses by members of such groups were specifically discussed and illustrated at this point prior to their detailed presentation in Part III. This may enable readers to define their purposes more clearly and to approach the study of the lists with some appropriate procedures in mind.

The Key Function of Local Administrative Leaders

In many county and community school systems today the improvement of the instructional program is a cooperative effort involving many persons, including students. Nevertheless, in most school systems the general use of a study such as this depends in large part upon the concern of the administrative and

47

supervisory groups for improvements in the high school's general education program and upon their willingness to join with the teaching staff in examining the study. Individual teachers or small groups of teachers are likely to make some use of it, but its general use in a school system or a high school will call for organized effort on the part of those in positions of leadership. This report follows the lead of some of the national professional organizations with whose work most of these administrators and supervisors are familiar. It undertakes to make specific the more general statements of functional objectives which these organizations have issued. It would seem, therefore, that leaders in many school systems would find here implementation for the general objectives to which they and the teachers subscribe. However, tradition and inertia in the secondary school being what they are, continuous adaptation of the program to the modern day and to the needs of unselected student bodies will not proceed as rapidly as it should unless stimulated by the wholehearted participation of local school leaders.

One way in which such leaders could encourage local professional personnel, lay groups, or students to use the results of this study would be a re-evaluation of the existing program of general education. Many school systems and high schools have one or more committees that are responsible for the improvement of all or some special part of the school's curriculum. Most curriculum committees have as their responsibility a particular subject or the courses in a certain department. Some schools have committees keyed to general purposes, such as health or citizenship, without reference to particular subjects or departments. Where an effort to develop a more integrated program of general education through some type of "core" or "block" program has been made, a school may have a committee in charge of the improvement of general education. However, it is believed that not many high schools or school systems have a faculty committee whose specific task is the improvement of the school's general education program and, therefore, a new committee charged with responsibility for study of this program may be needed. A study of Part I, where the importance of attaining the best possible results from general education is pointed out, where the weaknesses of most existing programs are reviewed, and where the reasons for setting goals in terms of changes in students' behaviors are discussed, might lead to the conviction that a committee empowered to make an evaluation of the school's existing program of general education ought to be created.

Such an evaluation, to be of the most service, ought to be made in terms of the achievement of the behavioral outcomes of the school's general education program which are considered by qualified observers to be the most important. It would also be helpful to secure their opinions as to how well the school is achieving those outcomes. Part III presents a plan (pages 214 to 229) that will enable individual members of such a group to indicate on a five-point scale how important they consider the outcomes proposed in this study to be for a particular high school and also to record their opinion as to whether the school is making as much effort as it should to achieve each outcome. It is not, of course, always possible to tell to what degree the school is responsible for any high levels of achievement shown because other factors may account for them. But where low levels of achievement are indicated, the school has reason to ask itself whether it should attempt to improve the situation by revising the program. It might also be helpful to invite groups of teachers, of parents of students, and of the older students to engage in independent evaluative studies and to participate in conferences at which the composite evaluations are discussed.

If such an evaluation were instituted or encouraged by local professional leaders, the findings should be presented to the whole high school faculty, and to the Board of Education and, hence, to the community. It should be used as a reason for undertaking such specific tasks of program improvement as were revealed to be desirable. This would require either an expansion of the function of the teachers' committee responsible for this evaluation or the creation of one or more new committees to develop new teaching plans designed to produce high levels of behavioral competence where the evaluation indicated them to be needed. If a school has committees for all the major purposes

49

of secondary education, new committees will not be needed since tasks appropriate to these purpose committees can become their responsibility. If a high school or system has several types of subject or departmental committees, each working rather independently in its particular area of the school's general education program, means must be found for coordinating the work of these committees. One plan might be to create a curriculum committee responsible for improving the work in all required courses included in the general education program and to leave to the subject or departmental committees the responsibility for other courses in each department which are not a part of the school's general education program. Another plan might be to retain the assigned scope of the work of these various departmental or subject committees but ask each of them to designate a representative to participate in an interdepartmental committee, to be known as the general education committee. This committee should then have responsibility for a continuous evaluation of the general education program-offerings in all departments and for proposals for improving them. When properly approved, these suggestions could be developed and put into effect by the appropriate subject or departmental committee. These committees jointly should be responsible for studying the problem of instructional materials and for developing broad lists of materials which would go far beyond the usual texts, for suggesting uses of community resources, and for proposing activities that would call for responsible student participation in their education.

Use by Interested Lay Groups

Although it is suggested above that laymen be asked by school leaders to participate in the process of curriculum improvement, there is no intention of implying that lay groups cannot institute such efforts on their own initiative. In many communities lay organizations are serving in a significant way to help the school study its problems. It is recognized that the school cannot go far toward the solution of the difficult problems without the active participation of such groups. To proceed otherwise invites public criticism and loss of the support essential to the school's welfare.

Instead of lay concern for the curriculum being characterized by individual, and often irresponsible, proposals for curriculum change, much would be gained if the interested persons would study the school's problems in an organized way. Such committees ought to be truly representative of lay interest in the school and should recognize that legal control of the school is exercised by the community through its Board of Education. A lay committee can, however, be of real help to the Board and its administrative officers if its members will devote enough time to make a thorough study and to become well informed in the area undertaken.

Communities are usually much interested in the behaviors of high school students and graduates. They do not hold the school responsible for all these behaviors nor do they want it to be. They hope and usually expect, however, that its program will help its students adopt good standards of behavior and attain, by the time they graduate, levels of behavioral competence desired of those approaching young adulthood. This report consists of proposals for use in general education in high school that are aimed at facilitating and encouraging student growth toward the more mature and more intelligent behaviors which many laymen find desirable. The question in any particular school is, What specific kinds and levels of competence on the part of students is the community most interested in having its high school program help to produce? A considered answer to this question, developed over a period of time by a representative lay group working in close cooperation with the school's staff, will provide better proposals for program improvement than is provided by individuals' "off the cuff" comments or by hastily developed group recommendations. The evaluative form appearing at the end of Part III could well be used by such a lay committee in its study of the high school's program. The committee will probably need a period of orientation prior to the use of this form. This could be accomplished perhaps by meetings in which the first two parts of this report are studied. The orientation period should lead to a common recognition by all committee members of what the term "general education" means, of what subjects the present program requires of all students, of what the function and scope of such a program are; and to familiarity with the evaluative form, how it was developed and can be used. This process will take some time but, as already suggested, unless a lay committee is willing to devote time to becoming well informed on a problem, its study is not likely to lead to conclusions which either it or the community will respect.

The use of this evaluative form by the committee would mean that, after the group had become somewhat oriented to the problem of general education, the members would evaluate independently each behavioral outcome appearing on the form as "highly important," "of some importance," "of little importance," or "omit" *as an area to be dealt with by the local high school's general education program*. The illustrative behaviors which appear under each subheading in the lists of proposed behavioral outcomes in Part III will give the group an idea of what is contemplated by each heading, and the group-judgment reached would then reflect what informed lay opinion in the community can be expected to support, as well as what it does not think is essential in that community. Each example was evaluated as of "high" or "some" importance to high schools by three-fourths or more of the contributing professional and lay groups. If a local lay committee will follow this same plan and consolidate the individual reports into a composite report, supported by three-fourths of the committee, it can then determine the relative importance attached to each outcome by the committee as a whole as it pertains to the particular community and its high school. Where three-fourths of the lay committee members agree that a particular outcome is important, it can be assumed that it represents a matter to which the high school's general education program should give serious consideration. If the committee places a low evaluation on an outcome, or if many check it to be omitted, it probably represents an outcome considered to be of little value in that community. Users of the form will note that it also provides an opportunity to express an opinion on whether the high school is making a satisfactory effort to achieve each outcome. This will indicate lay opinion as to the school's success in achieving these behaviors.

Committee members should be aware that this report contains many more proposals than will appeal to any one community or are needed by the students of any one school. These proposals represent a considered and double-checked list of outcomes for high schools generally, from which each high school and its community can select those that seem most important to it, and to which it can add others if this seems desirable. However, the fact that these proposals have been so strongly supported by professional and lay groups should induce a local committee to give each one careful consideration. Such an evaluation by an independent lay committee should be of real value to a high school staff, since it would then have some concrete assurance both of approval of the results being secured from the existing program and of desired directions of change.

Classroom Use by Individual Teachers

Whether or not a high school undertakes a broad evaluation and thorough-going reconstruction of its program of general education, individual teachers whose assignment includes required general education classes may find it both interesting and rewarding to review their teaching in the light of some of these proposed behavioral outcomes. General education in most high schools tends to center in required courses in English, mathematics, science, and the social sciences, all taught as separate subjects. In some other schools a more "integrated" offering of subjects exists with the subject orientation reduced. The particular uses that teachers of either of these types of programs may feel inclined to make of the results of this study will depend in part upon their concern about such questions as the following:

1. What kinds of competence does the school and its community expect from students taking any given subject or series of subjects in the school's required general education program? From a particular teacher or from a certain department? What is the defensible minimum in terms of objectives of the program? What will be recognized as a superlative result?

2. What kinds and levels of behaviors does the teacher or a department accept as essential for all students to strive for in

the courses for which a teacher or the department assumes responsibility? What do students think should be expected from all?

3. Which headings and subheadings in the lists of behavioral outcomes (Part III) seem to be of primary concern to the teacher, the department, or the community?

4. Which of the illustrations of behavior under these subheadings seem to be most closely related to the concerns of the teacher, the department, or the students?

5. How should these examples be modified to be more appropriate to a particular school and community?

6. What instruction is now offered (content and method) that tends to develop and encourage these specified kinds of behavioral competence and how might instruction be modified to increase the effort to build such competence?

7. Considering the students' community and family backgrounds and their native endowments, what kinds and levels of the illustrative behaviors can a particular course or sequence of courses in a general education program be expected to attain with its younger, less mature students? With its older, more mature students?

These questions assume that a teacher of general education classes is concerned with improving the level of behavioral competence resulting from the work in these classes. If this is not the case, perhaps Part I will help to show why there is public concern for such outcomes and why possession of knowledge alone does not give assurance that behavioral competence has been attained. When a teacher is inclined to accept behavioral outcomes as the most important results of his teaching, he is ready to examine the proposed outcomes and the illustrations to be found in Part III, and to select those which he can use in his courses. If the opinion of students is sought on this point, it may be necessary to convince them that high levels of some kinds of behavioral competence are just as reasonable expectations from general education courses as is improved ability to use a typewriter in a typing course. Once this point is understood, students' reactions to the lists of behaviors and student selection of those appropriate for a particular course may result in a wholly new approach to a course by them and the teacher. This development is likely to produce a need for different kinds of, and a greater variety of, instructional materials and a reassignment of time to various aspects of the course. Different ways of evaluating students' work in the course will be required, since acceptance of behavioral outcomes as desired results requires more information than how much knowledge is retained, and shifts attention to the question of how well students use knowledge and how they apply it to situations calling for a decision in regard to what course of action should be followed. Any individual teacher may find some worthwhile uses for some of the materials contained in this report as a way of improving his instruction, irrespective of whether or not the faculty collectively is interested in using it as a basis for curriculum improvement.

There is every reason why teachers responsible for instruction in required general education programs should try to reach answers to such questions as presented above. The answers will not be the same for all teachers nor for all schools. They will not be exactly the same next year for any teacher or school as they were this year. But if thoughtful consideration continues to be given to content, methods, and results, changes in the ends as well as the means of instruction may come about as the school and community observe the result of the efforts of the school to modify students' behaviors. It is not important that each teacher get exactly the same results as others; that each high school get the same results or that the results each year be the same. What is important is that every teacher and every school know what kinds of growth and development are sought through their general education program and that they seek for evidence of the success of their efforts in the changed and improved behavioral competence of the students. Tyler, in Chapter 12 of Part I of the Fifty-Second Yearbook of the National Society for the Study of Education, deals with the problem of translating youth needs into teaching goals.[1] For example, if a school and community feel that

[1] *Adapting the Secondary-School Program to the Needs of Youth:* Fifty-Second Yearbook, Part I. University of Chicago Press, Chicago, 1953, pp. 215–229.

problem-solving and critical thinking are of great importance in that school, a teaching goal has been established and kinds of behaviors related to it can be sought. Then content can be selected and used to encourage opportunity to develop these behaviors. This also applies if group participation or respect for human personalities are selected as points of major emphasis. Goals are thus established, kinds of behavior are indicated, and content and method are adjusted to conform to the realization of these goals. The scope of general education in high school, and its overriding functions as stressed in this report, set priorities for high schools in general. These priorities tend to be constant for all high schools, but each school and community has the responsibility of deciding what particular behavioral competencies are most important for it to seek, and of selecting the best means in content and method for developing these competencies.

The Objectives of Secondary Education and Behavioral Outcomes

These overall priorities exist because American high schools and their communities subscribe pretty generally to certain objectives for secondary education. General education is responsible for the achievement of some aspects of these objectives by all high school students and the elective, specialized offerings are responsible for carrying on this task for some of these students according to their aptitudes and interests. General education is largely depended upon in most high schools for attaining basic common aspects of the objectives of self-realization, human relationships, economic efficiency and civic responsibility, to use the classification popularized by the Educational Policies Commission.[1] Certain subjects are required of all in most high schools because they are expected to contribute to these goals. To use this report easily and effectively, high school teachers must be able to see the relationships between the objectives of secondary education which they and laymen so generally accept and the behavioral outcomes proposed here. It will also be helpful if each teacher can see which

[1] Educational Policies Commission, *The Purposes of Education in American Democracy*. National Education Association, Washington, 1938.

outcomes are most closely related to the subject he is teaching. We might merely encourage teachers to examine the proposals in Part III and make their own selections. But to simplify the process, the following four tables have been prepared to show the relationships of some of the principal objectives and some of the most commonly required subjects to the behavioral outcomes proposed. The subjects and school experiences which are generally relied upon for their achievement are listed. These are followed by proposed behavioral outcomes which ought to be evident if the objectives are being achieved. The pages in Part III on which these proposals appear, accompanied by examples, are listed for each behavioral outcome so that any teacher can easily determine what is implied.

TABLE 1-A. THE OBJECTIVES OF SELF-REALIZATION

The Inquiring Mind. The educated person has an appetite for learning.

Speech. The educated person can speak the mother tongue clearly.

Reading. The educated person reads the mother tongue efficiently.

Number. The educated person solves his problems of counting and calculating.

Sight and Hearing. The educated person is skilled in listening and observing.

Health Knowledge. The educated person understands the basic facts concerning health and disease.

Health Habits. The educated person protects his own health and that of his dependents.

Public Health. The educated person works to improve the health of the community.

Recreation. The educated person is participant and spectator in many sports and other pastimes.

Intellectual Interests. The educated person has mental resources for the use of leisure.

Aesthetic Interests. The educated person appreciates beauty.

Character. The educated person gives responsible direction to his own life.[1]

[1] Educational Policies Commission, *The Purposes of Education in American Democracy*. National Education Association, Washington, 1938, p. 50.

CAPITALIZING THE RESULTS OF THIS STUDY

TABLE 1-B. BEHAVIORAL OUTCOMES

ASPECTS OF A GENERAL EDUCATION PROGRAM EXPECTED TO CON-
TRIBUTE TO THESE OBJECTIVES: READING, COMPOSITION, SPELLING,
TYPEWRITING, ARITHMETIC, APPLIED MATHEMATICS, SHOPWORK,
HOMEMAKING, SCIENCES, HEALTH, HYGIENE, PHYSICAL EDUCATION,
SOCIAL STUDIES, PSYCHOLOGY, GUIDANCE, DRIVER EDUCATION,
SCHOOL ACTIVITIES, AND ORGANIZATIONS

PART III SUBHEADINGS		PAGES
1.11	Improving His Study Habits, Study Skills, and Other Work Habits	92 to 96
1.12	Improving in His Ability to Communicate and to Recognize and Use Good Standards	96 to 100
1.13	Becoming Sensitive to, and Competent in, the Use of Logical Thinking and Problem-Solving Processes	100 to 102
1.24	Improving in Ability to Apply Ethical Values as Gained from Religion, Philosophy, and Direct Experience to His Own Decisions and Behavior	108 to 110
1.25	Developing Aesthetic and Artistic Appreciations	110 to 112
1.31	Improving in Understanding and Control of Emotional Self	112 to 114
1.32	Improving in Understanding and Control of Physical Self	115 to 117
1.33	Showing Intelligent Use of Accepted Health Practices, and Wise Action on Health Problems	117 to 120
1.34	Making Intelligent Use of Accepted Safety Practices	120 to 122
2.31	Maintaining Health in the Home	156 to 158
2.32	Maintaining Health as a Participant in Small Peer-Groups	158 to 161
2.33	Contributing to Health and Safety in Small Group Situations in School and Community	162 to 163
3.11	Becoming Intellectually Able to Follow Developments on the World and National Levels and to Formulate Opinions About Proposed Solutions to Some of the Principal Problems and Issues	171 to 177
3.22	Developing Cultural Background Through Reading and Participating in Various Cultural Organizations and Activities	188 to 190
3.31	Recognizing Health as a World Problem and Supporting World-wide Scientific and Humanitarian Efforts and Organizations	191 to 193
3.32	Appreciating and Supporting Work and Services of Federal, State, and Local Health and Safety Departments, and of Volunteer Organizations	194 to 198

59

TABLE 2-A. THE OBJECTIVES OF HUMAN RELATIONSHIPS

Respect for Humanity. The educated person puts human relationships first.

Friendships. The educated person enjoys a rich, sincere, and varied social life.

Cooperation. The educated person can work and play with others.

Courtesy. The educated person observes the amenities of social behavior.

Appreciation of the Home. The educated person appreciates the family as a social institution.

Conservation of the Home. The educated person conserves family ideals.

Homemaking. The educated person is skilled in homemaking.

Democracy in the Home. The educated person maintains democratic family relationships.[1]

[1] Educational Policies Commission, *The Purposes of Education in American Democracy*, p. 72.

CAPITALIZING THE RESULTS OF THIS STUDY

TABLE 2-B. BEHAVIORAL OUTCOMES

ASPECTS OF GENERAL EDUCATION PROGRAM EXPECTED TO CONTRIB-
UTE TO THESE OBJECTIVES: JUNIOR HIGH SCHOOL SOCIAL STUDIES,
HOMEMAKING, CHILD-CARE, HEALTH, HYGIENE, CONSUMER EDUCA-
TION, ENGLISH, ECONOMICS, AMERICAN HISTORY, PROBLEMS OF
AMERICAN DEMOCRACY, GUIDANCE, STUDENT ACTIVITIES AND OR-
GANIZATIONS

61

TABLE 3-A. THE OBJECTIVES OF ECONOMIC EFFICIENCY

Work. The educated producer knows the satisfaction of good workmanship.

Occupational Information. The educated producer understands the requirements and opportunities for various jobs.

Occupational Choice. The educated producer has selected his occupation.

Occupational Efficiency. The educated producer succeeds in his chosen vocation.

Occupational Adjustment. The educated producer maintains and improves his efficiency.

Occupational Appreciation. The educated producer appreciates the social value of his work.

Personal Economics. The educated person plans the economics of his own life.

Consumer Judgment. The educated consumer develops standards for guiding his expenditures.

Efficiency in Buying. The educated consumer is an informed and skillful buyer.

Consumer Protection. The educated consumer takes appropriate measures to safeguard his interests.[1]

[1] Educational Policies Commission, *The Purposes of Education in American Democracy*, p. 90.

CAPITALIZING THE RESULTS OF THIS STUDY

TABLE 3-B. BEHAVIORAL OUTCOMES

ASPECTS OF A GENERAL EDUCATION PROGRAM EXPECTED TO CON-
TRIBUTE TO THESE OBJECTIVES: APPLIED MATHEMATICS, CONSUMER
EDUCATION, COMMUNITY CIVICS, SCIENCES, JUNIOR HIGH SCHOOL
SOCIAL STUDIES, AMERICAN HISTORY, ECONOMICS, HOMEMAKING,
PROBLEMS OF AMERICAN DEMOCRACY, GUIDANCE

TABLE 4-A. THE OBJECTIVES OF CIVIC RESPONSIBILITY

Social Justice. The educated citizen is sensitive to the disparities of human circumstance.

Social Activity. The educated citizen acts to correct unsatisfactory conditions.

Social Understanding. The educated citizen seeks to understand social structures and social processes.

Critical Judgment. The educated citizen has defenses against propaganda.

Tolerance. The educated citizen respects honest differences of opinion.

Conservation. The educated citizen has a regard for the nation's resources.

Social Applications of Science. The educated citizen measures scientific advance by its contribution to the general welfare.

World Citizenship. The educated citizen is a cooperating member of the world community.

Law Observance. The educated citizen respects the law.

Economic Literacy. The educated citizen is economically literate.

Political Citizenship. The educated citizen accepts his civic duties.

Devotion to Democracy. The educated citizen acts upon an unswerving loyalty to democratic ideals.[1]

[1] Educational Policies Commission, *The Purposes of Education in American Democracy*, p. 108.

CAPITALIZING THE RESULTS OF THIS STUDY

TABLE 4-B. BEHAVIORAL OUTCOMES

ASPECTS OF A GENERAL EDUCATION PROGRAM EXPECTED TO CON-
TRIBUTE TO THESE OBJECTIVES: SCHOOL ACTIVITIES AND ORGANIZA-
TIONS, JUNIOR HIGH SCHOOL SOCIAL STUDIES, HOMEMAKING, COM-
MUNITY CIVICS, AMERICAN HISTORY, PROBLEMS OF AMERICAN DE-
MOCRACY, SCIENCE, ECONOMICS, CONSUMER EDUCATION, ENGLISH,
GUIDANCE

PART III
SUBHEADINGS   PAGES

1.21   Revealing the Personal Understandings and Characteristics of   103 to 104
        the Good Citizen

1.22   Attaining a Perspective on Present-Day Events, Cultures, and   104 to 106
        Conditions

1.23   Attaining Orientation to the Physical World and Appreciation   106 to 108
        of What Scientific Advancements Mean to the World

2.43   Manifesting Interest and Participation in the Economic Affairs   169 to 170
        of the Community

3.11   Becoming Intellectually Able to Follow Developments on the   171 to 177
        World and National Levels and to Formulate Opinions About
        Proposed Solutions to Some of the Principal Problems and
        Issues

3.13   Evidencing Intelligent Appreciation and Support of Democratic   182 to 185
        Goals and Principles and of American Cultural, Social, and
        Political Traditions

3.21   Viewing Current Events and Conditions in This Country and in   186 to 188
        the World in the Light of Their Historic and Cultural Pasts

3.23   Seeing Vocational Activities in Their Cultural Settings   190 to 191

3.31   Recognizing Health as a World Problem, and Supporting   191 to 193
        Worldwide Scientific and Humanitarian Efforts and Organi-
        zations

3.42   Supporting Measures of Federal, State, and Local Govern-   203 to 204
        ment, and Voluntary Organizations Designed to Conserve
        Human and Natural Resources

3.43   Understanding the Need for Federal and State Governments'   205 to 208
        Stimulative and Regulatory Activities in Economic Matters and
        Affairs as Means of Making Our Free Enterprise System Work

65

The foregoing tables provide a quick reference point for teachers' curriculum committees responsible for the attainment of any one of these objectives in a high school. They can also be used by the teachers of any department or subject in appraising their present courses. Conferences of such groups of teachers should decide what responsibility each subject has for each outcome and should allocate major and minor responsibilities to particular teachers or subjects. This would provide more assurance than now exists in many high schools that the instructional program is actually covering an accepted general objective as fully as it should. The effort here is to develop clearer perceptions of what happens if these objectives are achieved, and of the responsibility of certain required subjects for helping to achieve them. It will be observed that some of these subjects appear in successive tables. This is as it should be, for it tends to emphasize the point that these subjects are not separate, isolated entities but are interrelated parts of a general education program with recognized objectives toward which they can and should make major contributions. If any subject can make a major contribution to but one objective, it should probably be found only among the school's elective specialized offerings. The reason these subjects (and their contents reorganized into a "core") have become the required general education program and are allowed to continue as such lies in the fact that they can be so taught as to make real contributions to several of these objectives of general education. The chief factor in determining whether these possibilities are achieved or not lies in the use a teacher and his students decide to make of the content of general education courses. The full measure of their potentialities is achieved, however, only when there is cooperative planning by all teachers of all general education classes in a high school, so that general education in that school actually is a *program* and not merely a collection of isolated courses.

These four tables may be particularly useful to readers whose interests center in a particular general education subject. To serve the purpose of other readers who may want to get an overview of the results of the entire study without all the details, it is suggested that the evaluative form previously mentioned may be used. It lists the main headings and subheadings under which the illustrative behaviors are grouped, but does not include the latter or the "developmental equivalents." This results in a short form or synopsis of the results of the study and yet, since page references for each subheading are provided, it is relatively easy for the reader to study any details that may be of interest. This synopsis also permits a reader who wants to get an overview of any one field of growth (self-realization, for example) to do so merely by following through the successive pages devoted to this growth-field, thus covering the 1.1, 1.2, 1.3, and 1.4 clusters of behaviors. If, on the other hand, one wants to follow through one *area* of competence (becoming culturally oriented and integrated, for example) he can pick out the sections of the synopsis numbered 1.2, 2.2, and 3.2 and discover what is included under this area in each of the growth-fields.

Use of Results in Guidance and Testing

In Counseling and Guidance. Those in charge of guidance activities in a school, including class teachers with official guidance responsibilities, should be especially sensitive to the effect on students' behaviors of a given program of general education. It can be expected that they will approach their responsibilities with an eye to the all-round growth and development of students and to good and bad effects of this required program. They can be expected to recognize that behavior is always caused; that a school and its program do affect the behavior of individuals and of groups whether the school consciously intends to do so or not. Since guidance workers are concerned for the all-round growth of personality and are in positions where lack of adjustment between pupils and their programs is brought to their attention and where program-planning for students is often done, they should react favorably to proposals that the high school program be primarily concerned with encouraging and facilitating desirable modifications of behavior in students. They will probably welcome a statement of general education goals which is based on the assumption that changes in behavior should be the major outcomes of this program and which suggests some of the principal areas of behavior that should be taken into account, if in the process of curriculum improvement, the mental health and the emotional stability of the student are to be considered. As they counsel with individual students, guidance workers often uncover emotional pressures created by program requirements which seem unreasonable and pointless to these students. If the required subjects were organized for the purpose of encouraging desirable and useful behavioral competence and this purpose were seen by the student, maladjustment to the required subject, in many instances, would be removed.

If a high school were committed to this approach to general education, it would be much more likely that, when the guidance personnel reported undesirable situations to class teachers, attempts would be made to remove the pressure points and make the courses more effective means of promoting the desirable growth and development of students. Instead of the teacher being inclined to maintain that the subject matter under discussion was essential to the mastery of the subject, the question would be, Is the subject matter essential to the well-rounded growth and development and, hence, to the behavioral competence of students? A "guidance approach" to class teaching would thus be stimulated and the school's whole general education program would tend to become *behavior-centered* rather than subject-centered. Mastery of content would be no less important but the basis for deciding what content should be mastered would be changed.

Another use which guidance workers might find for this report would be in stimulating the improvement of the school's pupil-personnel records. Too many of these records now tend to emphasize only what the student knows and neglect to stress what kind of person he is or what he can do. The trend in the improvement of these records has been toward broadening them and toward including objective and descriptive comments on how well students use course content where it is appropriate to do so. Colleges are increasingly interested in receiving records from high schools which give a broader and sounder base for judging a student's potentialities than they obtain from records concerned almost exclusively with course marks. Parents used to getting the conventional "grade" card often are slow to accept a report which substitutes more descriptive, and to them less definitive, statements about their children's work. When these latter statements are supplementary to a mark, there is less objection and many parents are learning of their value and also of the value of teacher-parent conferences as a part of the school's pupil personnel practices. A program of general education which stresses behavioral competence makes conventional pupil-personnel record forms inappropriate, or at least inadequate, records of what the school professes to be most concerned about. Wrinkle's account[1] of the efforts of the College High School of the Colorado State College of Education at Greeley to develop more adequate bases for evaluating the work of pupils is the classic example of the success of (and difficulty encountered in) an effort by teachers, students, and parents to reach a common understanding of what the school's goals should be, and to agree upon a satisfactory way of reporting to parents the progress of a pupil toward these goals. Inspection of these records shows how getting and using knowledge are woven together to form a basis for evaluating the success of a student. This account also shows how other pupil-personnel records and practices were affected when a school recognized changed behavior as the purpose of education and tried to make its program and administration, as well as its personnel records, consistent with this purpose. To the extent that this idea of centering a program upon the growth and development of students toward more mature behavior is accepted by class teachers, students, and parents, a better understanding of the work of the school's guidance staff can be developed and progress toward both a better program and better pupils' records accelerated.

The full acceptance of improved behavior as the outcome of education will also result in more interest on the part of the whole school staff in the early discovery of pupils' aptitudes and inter-

[1] Wrinkle, William L., *Improving Marking and Reporting Practices.* Rinehart and Co., New York, 1947.

ests. A program of general education concerned chiefly with behavioral outcomes is bound to influence a staff to recognize content and method as means toward desired ends rather than ends in themselves. They are impelled toward observing the effects of their teaching and in the end come to know, and are interested in knowing, more about the aptitudes and interests of their students than is presently the case with teachers of the required program in most high schools. This increased knowledge and interest in pupils serves to improve the counsel these teachers are able to give students about their high school work and programs and their post-high school careers. If the staff has available appropriate comprehensive cumulative records, it can supply parents, colleges, and employers with more reliable and pertinent information about its students than schools are usually able to provide.

In Testing and Assessment. One of the functions of a good guidance staff (or of the principal in case the school has no specialized guidance worker) is to help the teachers develop a testing program which indicates something of the success of the instructional program and how the program can be improved. Many of the proposals for the use of this report can be carried out most effectively when we have testing and evaluative instruments which reveal, better than any now available, the levels and kinds of behavioral competence possessed by high school students and graduates. Teachers could then secure a better idea of the results of present programs of general education and gain insights into how to strengthen them. Such tests also would show the effectiveness of program changes in terms of behavioral competence. These tests would not only evaluate existing programs, diagnosing strengths and weaknesses, but would also furnish more reliable evidence of the results of curriculum change than we now have.

Testing agencies have already developed some tests which tend to show probable ability to behave appropriately if faced with responsibilities in a certain area of performance. These tests also tend to show whether the actual performance or behavior of a person when confronted with these responsibilities is appropriate or not. For the most part such tests deal with somewhat narrow areas of behavior, such as in a particular position in business, industry, or government service. The tendency, however, is toward developing tests for use in connection with broader and more complex situations. Most of such test development has been applied to nonschool situations, or to such areas of specialized education as are represented at the secondary school level by elective subjects and at the higher education level by programs of professional education. They have not yet been developed for use in such general areas as citizenship or economic competence, for example.

This report, however, is a step in the direction of developing such tests in the general education area. Before this can be done those who are engaged in test development activities must have some specific ideas about what kinds and levels of behavioral competence are accepted as desirable and reasonable for secondary schools to attempt to encourage, facilitate, and establish. The report gives in some detail examples of behavioral competence which carefully selected professional and lay groups believe to be the objectives of general education in high school. On the basis of the use of the results of this report and their refinement through such use, batteries of tests may be developed which will give high schools a much better measure of the effectiveness of their programs of general education in terms of behavioral competence than they now have. Such tests would be helpful in evaluating the relative effectiveness of various general education subjects when taught in various ways and of the "subject-organized" programs of general education as a whole in comparison with such more "integrated," "core," or "block" types of programs. At present we have little concrete evidence of results on which to base claims for any of the various plans of organizing general education. If this report can be a means of helping to develop such testing and evaluating instruments, perhaps it will mark a distinctive step toward making the declared functional objectives of secondary education more of a reality.

Since the first step in the process of developing a good program of evaluation is a listing of objectives, this report has obvious implications for the improvement of measurement. Once the curriculum has been planned and organized in terms of specific behavioral goals, the broad design for the best testing program for that curriculum has been indicated. The curriculum, stated as a series of behavioral objectives, determines *what* should be measured in any evaluation of student progress and school accomplishment, and goes a long way in suggesting *how* achievement should be measured.

If the report is to be used for the improvement of testing (or for the improvement of anything else of importance in the school), the first need is that of providing copies enough for everyone on the staff. The teachers, obviously, are the first members of the staff who should receive copies. One may assume that a thorough perusal of the report by teachers is necessary before it can be used widely in curriculum planning. Study and discussion of the report by the teachers, then, will serve the purpose of *both* curriculum planning and test design. Another step already suggested is also necessary for both curriculum and testing work—the determination by teachers, administrators, and lay community of just which outcomes are to be sought by the school. These first steps, shared by both curriculum planners and test-builders, are prerequisite for good measurement. The important point is that what are to be the results of teaching and what is to be tested, should be determined at the same time by the same people. Only when this is done can measurement be made to "fit" the curriculum in a way to afford the most useful outcomes for testing.

Once the behavioral goals for individuals and classes have been agreed upon by all those concerned, a teaching group should decide which outcomes should be tested schoolwide by the administrator or guidance officer, and which outcomes should be tested by the teachers in situations limited to single classes. That is, there are certain outcomes which the school seeks for all its students and which can be tested best in a schoolwide evaluation. These usually are the "basic skills," the "common learnings" for which both the school and the community wish to set desirable minimum standards for all students, and to evaluate broadly as a means of assessing the effectiveness of the school in its instructional program. These schoolwide tests can be supplemented by such individual class tests as a teacher may need in order to gain a more intimate picture of growth of his or her particular group.

Whether testing techniques are to be used by the teacher with a single class of students, or by the school with all its students, the successive steps in test-building and application follow the same rules. The second step for both teacher and administrator (better yet, the teacher and administrator cooperating in a design for testing procedures) is a decision on the methods to be used in evaluation. Some kinds of teaching goals are amenable to measurement with paper and pencil tests. Ability to use many of the academic skills of reading, writing, number manipulation, and the recall of information are tested best and most economically with instruments of a fairly ordinary kind—both the objective and essay types. The outcomes suggested by this report, with those sought by the particular school marked or otherwise identified, can be used effectively in this second step simply by screening out those things which teachers and administrators believe can be tested with some validity by means of paper and pencil tests. In this application, the report will help to remind educators that many goals of instruction are amenable to ordinary testing practices, but that many others are not.

A third step, once the outcomes to be measured in traditional ways have been identified and set aside for developmental work, is the identification of behavioral goals for which special kinds of evaluative techniques need to be developed. Since the sought-for outcomes of instruction are stated in behavioral terms, this report will help teachers recognize the importance of observation of behavior for purposes of evaluation. If one of the agreed-upon goals of instruction is that of motivating and training students to play effective roles in group situations, then the only way in which students' growth toward this goal can be evaluated is by observation of students in group situations. Sometimes this behavior is exhibited in the classroom or in other school situations, but often it can be best exhibited only in out-of-school situations. Here the ingenuity of the educator is taxed to a greater degree.

Techniques for observing and recording behavior in the community at large, as well as in the home, are much more difficult to devise than paper and pencil tests—but they can be done and have been done.

The Eight-Year Study pointed out the desirability of the school's staff becoming alert to evidences of the achievement of the school's goals in out-of-class and out-of-school life, and suggested ways of noting and evaluating this type of evidence.[1] Actually, many high schools recognize the validity of this idea and show it by the time and attention they give to "extra-class activities" and the importance they attach to evidence of ability to participate successfully in these activities. If these activities are not important ways of developing competence to behave appropriately in group-situations, less time should be devoted to them. If they are effective in promoting this goal of general education, then they should be freely recognized by the school as a part of the school's general education program and results noted and recorded. So also with students' community activities. Since they are recognized as opportunities for developing desirable behavioral competence, they should be incorporated into the general education program and the results of participation as eagerly evaluated as are those commonly observed in the classroom.

Perhaps the main reason techniques for evaluating performance in extra-class and community activities lag behind those that have been developed for use in classroom situations lies in the school's reluctance to recognize actual and responsible participation by students in school and community activities as an integral part of the general education curriculum. If these techniques were as freely utilized in general education classes as they are in distributive education classes, for example, teachers would get better insights into how to test for behavioral competence. This report does not tell the teacher how observation of out-of-

[1] Smith, Eugene R., Ralph W. Tyler, and others, *Appraising and Recording Student Progress*, Harper and Bros., New York, 1942, chaps. 3 and 10. See also Jarvie, Lawrence L., and Mark Ellingson, *A Handbook on the Anecdotal Behavior Journal*, University of Chicago Press, Chicago, 1940; and Aikin, Wilford M., *The Story of the Eight-Year Study*, Harper and Bros., New York, 1942.

school behavior should be provided for, but its listing of the desirable outcomes ought to help, since it permits the teacher to see quite easily which goals will require this more difficult approach. Also, it ought to help teachers avoid accepting demonstration of skill in the learning exercise as a substitute for demonstration of the goal behavior. Beyond these points, however, the report offers little actual help in test design. It serves merely as a first guide toward those kinds of behavior which it is important to test in one way or another.

Beyond the point of design, though, the report may have considerable usefulness in setting up the content of evaluation. When the teacher can start with a specific list of desired performances, ideas for appropriate test tasks and questions come easily. Take a straightforward objective such as helping a group of tenth graders to learn to write better by pointing up the importance of the proper subordination of ideas or modifiers in a sentence. The learning exercises intended to aid in the development of good sentence sense may involve formal recognition of various kinds of clauses and phrases—the grammatical parts—although such recognition is not a real goal of instruction. In order to assess the progress of students toward the real instructional goal, the teacher must devise some writing situation that "puts the students on their own" because it makes them feel the need to write well and then see which students actually do write sentences in which the parts are properly subordinated. The list of outcomes, then, will help the teacher keep not only the curriculum but also the evaluation of growth focused on the out-put rather than on the in-put of instruction. One of the great faults of most teacher-made tests is that they tend to concentrate on a "playback" of learning materials. This report, as supplemented or amended in the local school, should help all educators concentrate on what is of most importance—the behavior of the student.

Still another use of the report in the improvement of evaluation is that afforded by the "developmental equivalents" of the behaviors which form a section of Part III. Even when the teacher is concentrating on the outcomes of instruction, it is necessary to know what kinds of behavior to look for along the way. Both

75

teaching and testing are cumulative in nature, so that even with the eyes set on more or less distant goals it is necessary to maintain checkpoints as students grow toward those goals. The developmental equivalents—reflecting the behavior of younger, less mature students as they develop desired skills and attitudes—thus will serve as guides in the construction of evaluative techniques for the younger students. Although both schools and individual students vary tremendously in rate of development toward desired goals, it can be generalized roughly that the developmental equivalents listed in this report probably will be useful in approaching the construction of evaluative devices for eighth and ninth graders, while the outcomes themselves will be most useful in setting up test situations for juniors and seniors.

Finally, this report will serve a useful purpose in the improvement of measurement if it does no more than bring the teaching staff together in groups for the consideration of what to test. Even in the schools where there are well-developed schoolwide testing programs, there is usually a tendency for any testing done beyond this program to be designed and accomplished by individual teachers. Any device or stratagem which can be employed to encourage teachers to work together in achieving outcomes of instruction is likely to be useful. Administrators and curriculum planners expect the school experience to be a continuous and integrated one for every pupil. In order for the school experience to have these characteristics, not only the teaching but also the testing should be designed and implemented in such a way that all of the parts contribute to the whole. Use of a single list of objectives, if properly managed by the school administration, can bring teachers together in such a way that their efforts at evaluation provide a more coherent and comprehensive coverage of goals than is now generally the case in evaluation.

Pending the development of more objective tests and the acquisition of improved testing techniques, however, we need not twiddle our curricular thumbs. There is much to be said for action in line with the considered opinions of informed groups. Much progress in many fields of human endeavor has resulted from action based on the best thinking of a well-informed person or group in a particular field. Science often serves as the hand-maiden of philosophy, coming along in due time to furnish objective proof of the wisdom of what the best thinkers in a field had arrived at on the basis of their professional reasoning and judgment. Often we are not content to stand still, continuing to do what, on the basis of our observations, we have less and less faith in. Self-respect requires that we try something which we believe may be better. It is at this point that many members of the profession find themselves with reference to general education in high school. We have long declared our allegiance to the general objectives set forth in the past fifty years both by lay and by professional groups. Many individual teachers and some school systems have implemented general objectives by modifying content, courses, and teaching methods. They have done this without the benefit of as much general agreement on specific kinds and levels of behavior as they could have used. If this report eventually helps in the development of better evaluative instruments for use in general education in high school and, in the interim, if it serves as a guide to schools that are now trying to develop better programs of general education, and test them as best they may, it will have served its two basic purposes.

Use by Other Educational Organizations and Institutions

So far Part II has been devoted to suggested uses of this report by local school systems, high schools, and communities. This section will cover some possibilities for use by nonlocal institutions. While the principal responsibility for the improvement of a high school's program of general education should continue to rest with the school's staff and community, helpful work has been, and can be, done by such regional agencies as the North Central Association, for example. It early manifested its interest in general education by initiating the work which led to the publication of *General Education in the American High School*, previously cited. This interest has been continued by subsequent association committee work. The effort of this association and of the other regional agencies to be of help to local high schools in their efforts at program improvement is also indicated by their interest in the development and use of *The Evaluative Criteria*.[1] The 1950 edition of this instrument includes for the first time some indication of the desirability of evaluating a high school in terms of its achievement of the general objectives of secondary education. For the most part, however, it concentrates upon evaluation of the conventional subjects as means toward the attainment of these objectives rather than upon student success in actually achieving them. Is it too much to expect that a 1960 edition could be developed which would take the proposed behavioral outcomes of this report (or modifications of them) as a basis for evaluating the general education programs of high schools? This would shift the evaluation of this aspect of a high school's responsibility to results in terms of its "out-put" and away from its "in-put." The real measure of the success of any organization is its product, not the materials it uses in the process. That there already is some organized effort on the part of some high schools to seek for better methods of evaluating their work than the 1950 edition of *The Evaluative Criteria* provides, is evidenced by the interest of the California Association of Secondary School Administrators in developing their own plan for use by schools in that state.

State Departments of Education. Much that has been said about the use of this report by local schools and school systems can be said in favor of its use by state departments of education in their efforts to help high schools improve their general education programs. Granted that the primary responsibility for this work lies with local school staffs, state departments of education exercise leadership functions which can be helpful to local schools engaged in the improvement of their instructional programs. Under its leadership, state professional and lay groups can develop general policies and proposals which operate as a guide and stimulus to local schools. A state lay committee, for example, could use it for the same purposes as a local lay committee. The members of a state department of education concerned with the secondary school curriculum could be responsible for the development of discussion groups of high school principals and teachers of the state where this report was the subject of discussion and where

[1] American Council on Education, *The Evaluative Criteria*. Washington, 1950.

some general curriculum policies for the state were agreed upon. These might lead to modifications or new interpretations of statewide program requirements which would provide more general agreement upon desired outcomes, new freedom of action for local high schools, and encouragement for curriculum changes in certain agreed-upon directions. Perhaps the most important effect might be in the further improvement of statewide testing programs in the states where these programs exist. These quite naturally influence instruction in the high school markedly and it is of utmost importance that this influence be such as to encourage and enable high schools more effectively to achieve the desired objectives of secondary education. What is said above about the improvement of testing procedures in local schools has pertinence also for those responsible for statewide testing programs.

Institutions That Prepare Teachers. Institutions of higher education that have the privilege of preparing and recommending for certification students for teaching in the secondary schools have a responsibility not only for preparing them for teaching in certain fields, but also for their orientation to the whole field of secondary education. Courses in curriculum organization and improvement are used to enable students to see how present concepts of the function of secondary education in the United States are affecting the curriculum and more specifically how the principles of learning can be used to make teaching more effective. The general objectives of secondary education are usually examined in such courses, and prospective teachers are urged to make their teaching contribute to their realization. This report should permit instructors of these courses to propose that the more specific outcomes suggested be utilized in planning content, methods, and out-of-class experiences for use in required general education courses in high school. Such use would be a corrective for the usual overemphasis in college courses upon knowledge as an end in itself in education. It might be a good thing if in some course each student-teacher planned, taught, and tested a learning unit suitable for use in a required general education course in which the purpose of the unit was to modify his students' behaviors in a

79

direction proposed by some behavioral outcomes included in this report. These college students would thus be brought face to face with the fact that whatever their future teaching assignments may be, their effectiveness as teachers will be largely determined by their ability to induce their students to acquire higher standards and levels of behavioral competence.

This report recognizes that general education does not begin or end in high school. It has recognized its relation to, and dependence upon, the report dealing with the objectives of the elementary school. It quotes freely from the general education literature developed by those interested in general education in college. It recognizes general education as a "seamless web" which has both length and breadth. It does not hold that it is the duty of secondary schools to reach the behavioral outcomes which it proposes. It maintains, however, that these schools should be teaching toward such outcomes. Much will remain to be done for many high school graduates in post-high school educational institutions. Instructors in junior, general, and liberal arts colleges who teach general education courses at the college level might well consider some of the outcomes proposed in this report and develop comparable lists of desirable outcomes for their courses, and then evaluate their courses to discover how effectively they are promoting these desirable modifications of student behavior. If the desired outcome of general education is modified behavior, as college general education leaders say, and if the proposed outcomes developed in this report are as valid as selected professional and lay groups think them to be, then they may have at least some pertinence for general education instructors in college.

With two reports on general education in elementary and secondary schools prepared by specialized professional workers at these two levels now completed, it might be a good thing if another study was undertaken by a group of college instructors of general education courses. It could well start with the statements of general objectives already prepared for use in college by distinguished groups of college representatives and with their commitment to behavior as the basic outcome of such courses. It could consider the outcomes proposed by the elementary and secondary school groups and adopt, modify, and extend its lists of college outcomes to meet the needs of a somewhat more selective and more mature group of students. We would then have three reports covering the full range of formal general education and perhaps achieve a more consistent and integrated approach to the full task of general education for American children and youth than at present. Following the publication of this third report, it is possible that a reviewing committee, composed of representatives of all levels of education from elementary to higher, should evaluate all three reports, pointing out their strong and weak spots and proposing such modifications as would produce as nearly as practicable the "seamless web" of general education which is admitted on theoretical grounds to be desirable.

Behavior-Centered General Education

It must have been perfectly obvious to readers long before now that this study hopes to help high schools develop what might be properly called behavior-centered general education programs which have as their goal building in youth the kinds of common competence they need to meet life's demands. As Thomas said in an article in *School and Society:*

> Competence is not made up of a bundle of isolated skills, facts, and appreciations tied together with a sheepskin like a set of golf clubs in a bag, any one of which may be pulled out and used on demand. Instead, facts, skills, and appreciations, all together make up a responsible selective judgment, the various facets of which are fused, complementary. No phase of selective judgment can be used without involving the whole of selective judgment—[it is a capacity] for wise response and action.[1]

Education for such competence, of course, is not a new idea in education. It is probably as old as education itself. It is an idea that is generally accepted by high schools and accounts for many of the innovations in their programs. It accounts for their expanded elective offerings. It is the best explanation for their interest in student activities which they still regard as "extra." It

[1] Thomas, W. Craig, "A Concept of General Education," *School and Society*, vol. 72, no. 1876, 1950, p. 357.

is revealed when high schools parade their most accomplished art, music, drama, speech, and athletic specimens before their publics and are glad to bask in the reflected glory of their demonstrations of achieved ability. It is shown when members of their honor societies are chosen not only because of their commendable levels of scholarship, but also because of their "service" and citizenship records. The graduates of their specialized vocational programs are required to show initial levels of competence in their chosen vocations. The graduates of an advanced, elective science course are expected to begin to exhibit the habits of thought and work which mark them as young scientists. One of the principal outcomes sought from extra-class activity programs is the ability and willingness to carry responsibility. There are many other reasons for believing that high schools are committed to the task of developing behavioral competence.

But somewhere along the line the general education program ran afoul of some sociological and psychological booby-traps which have prevented it from becoming an effective means for developing the unspecialized types of behavioral competence, the possession of which is just as important for all youth as are specialized behaviors for some students. Among these booby-traps are the propaedeutic theory of education, the cultural transmission idea, selective secondary education, education for leadership, formal discipline, and a misconception of what constitutes college preparation. The result has been that even though high schools readily accept and generally practice the idea that education ought to affect behavior, their programs of general education have not made the adaptations required if they are to be effective in producing the common behavioral competencies required of citizens, homemakers, and workers in today's world.

The use of the results of this study suggested here does not, therefore, require the development of a totally new and wholly different high school, for the principles underlying these proposals are being accepted and being partially applied in many existing schools. This report does propose, however, that a high school should become internally consistent, that it should make as direct an approach to the development of behavioral competence in its general education program as it now uses in its program of specialized education—that the school should build its whole educational program on one philosophical base and utilize the same psychological principles clear across the curricular board. The closing chapter of the Fifty-Second Yearbook of the National Society for the Study of Education[1] pictures a "youth-oriented" high school in which behavior-forming instruction is stressed. It does not call for a new educational institution, but it does indicate certain characteristics of present-day high schools whose importance would be enlarged if meeting the needs of youth and changing their behaviors became all-absorbing institutional concerns. In most high schools these characteristics exist in a more or less well-developed form. To become the "benign habitat" for the growth and development of all youth which a high school in America is supposed to be, each school needs to concentrate on developing the characteristics which contribute to the creation of such an environment and to sublimate those which interfere with it. All this report envisions is that high schools strive as hard and as intelligently to develop the characteristic which enable all youth to become competent in the important unspecialized areas of behavior as they now do to enable some youth to develop specialized kinds of competence. This can be done by developing general education programs specifically focused upon such important unspecialized behaviors as are proposed in this study. It will require the planning of activities, experiences, and projects which will provide opportunity for active, responsible student participation basic to the attainment of all behavioral competence.

No high school would have to undergo an institutional re-birth to do this. Any high school that has developed a good offering of specialized, elective courses and programs can do it. But if a high school really threw itself wholeheartedly into the task of developing such a general education program, it would cease to reveal the tendencies toward institutional schizophrenia which many

[1] National Society for the Study of Education, *Adapting The Secondary School Program to the Needs of Youth:* Fifty-Second Yearbook, Part I. University of Chicago Press, Chicago, 1953, pp. 296–312.

high schools now show when their specialized programs of education rather freely accept and generally use a philosophical base and a set of psychological principles which their general education program only halfheartedly and sporadically accepts and uses. Maybe this means that they would be born again!

Part III

ORGANIZATION OF PROPOSED
BEHAVIORAL OUTCOMES

This third section of the report presents in detail the work of the consultants and reviewers. It includes the lists of proposed behavioral outcomes of general education, illustrations of the various categories of behavior, and some suggested "developmental equivalents." As the staff and consultants approached the task of making these lists, they felt the need for developing a common framework to guide them. There was a distinct understanding that each consultant was free to use the framework as he wished, but there was enough agreement upon basic essentials so that a pattern acceptable to practically all members of the groups was developed. Since a knowledge of this pattern of organization will help the readers understand the rationale of the lists, this section opens with an explanation of it. The detailed lists of behaviors are then presented. Part III closes with a form to be used by high schools in evaluating their general education programs.

The organization of the lists of behaviors (see chart on pages 88–89) is built upon three directions of behavioral growth which all youth must make as they develop toward maturity in four areas where they must attain competence if they are to carry on the common activities of life in a manner satisfactory to themselves and acceptable to society. The three directions of growth are basic because they encompass the growth situations of life in which each youth is expected to learn to behave maturely. These "directions of growth" therefore appear at the top of the chart.

For the purpose of planning a program of educative experience in order to help youth grow toward maturity, the chart provides

85

four areas of behavioral competence, the main implications of which have been accepted in one form or another by many high schools. These "areas of behavioral competence" appear along the left side of the chart. An explanatory statement concerning each direction of growth and area of competence is provided. It is assumed that, if the school's general education program results in more competent behavior on the part of its students in these four areas and in the three directions of growth, it will be performing the functions expected of it. Thus, twelve broad groups of behaviors are represented by the rectangles on the chart. It is held that if one is to make desirable growth toward self-realization, for example, behavioral competence in all four areas must be developed. Likewise, if one becomes intellectually competent, it will be because of growth not only toward intellectual self-realization but also toward ability to participate intelligently in the activities and relationships of small groups, and in the responsibilities which devolve upon members and leaders of large organizations of various kinds. These twelve groups of behaviors are not mutually exclusive; they are consequently set off from each other by broken rather than solid lines. They served very well, however, as centers around which proposed behaviors could be clustered.

The proposed lists of behavioral outcomes, beginning on page 92, are arranged under headings and subheadings in groups which fall within the rectangles of the chart from 1.1 through 3.4. Under each heading examples of behavioral competence are provided to indicate more specifically what the consultants had in mind. It should be remembered that these are *illustrative* only and do not pretend to be inclusive. Nor are all behaviors proposed as essential in every high school. They represent proposals for high schools in general from which a particular school might choose those of special importance to it. These lists of examples are consolidations and condensations of those suggested by the consultants. Outcomes which were evaluated by 90 per cent of the reviewers as of "high" importance are indicated by an asterisk. Outcomes not followed by an asterisk were evaluated as of "high" or of "some" importance by at least 75 per cent of the reviewers. Outcomes proposed by the consultants which were not supported to this degree by the reviewers do not appear in the lists. Some of the behavioral outcomes were drawn from the previously mentioned elementary school study and were included here if they were also considered appropriate for junior or senior high schools by at least 75 per cent of the reviewers.

High Levels and Wide Ranges of Maturity Recognized

The outcomes are usually stated so as to represent a reasonable expectation for the most mature of high school seniors. No senior, of course, is equally mature in all respects and even the most mature cannot fully attain many of these outcomes. But perceptible growths toward such competence are proposed as desirable goals for general education. If these seem to set too high a standard for even the most mature seniors, perhaps it is well to remember how far above the typical adult the potential levels of competence to think, feel, and act—to behave—the best of our seniors are. If these proposed behaviors *seem* high and *are* high when compared to the behavioral competence now exhibited by this top group, perhaps we are unwittingly admitting that the present programs of general education are not producing the behavioral competence which this group has the power to reach.

The statement of these proposals in terms of high levels of expectation for the most mature of our older students is not intended to imply that the threshold of general education should be raised above that which can reasonably be expected of the less mature senior high school students or of younger students in junior high school. That some of the listed behaviors already are part of the thought and action patterns of some of the more mature high school students does not invalidate them as outcomes which ought to be sought for all those who have not attained them. Let us hope that a considerable number of the outcomes have been rather well attained by many high school students, either by reason of home training or previous schooling. But when some students of a high school do not exhibit the kinds of behaviors indicated by an outcome which has been accepted by it as important, then it is a matter of at least some importance for the school to stress this in its general education program.

Mature Behaviors in Older
Youth Manifest — — — — — →

1. **Growth Toward Self-Realization.** General education in high school should help youth develop the common kinds of behaviors indicative of such personal growth and development as will enable them within the limits of their native endowments, to live richer, more satisfying, more productive lives consonant with our ethical, aesthetic, and social standards and values.

To Be Willing and Able
to Manifest Mature Behaviors
as an Older Youth, Each High
School Student Must Be |
                          |
                          ↓

1. **Attaining Maximum Intellectual Growth and Development.** Behavioral outcomes to be sought from general education because the living of a satisfying personal life requires intellectual growth and development toward the limit of one's capacity.

1.1 Part III, pages 92 to 102

2. **Becoming Culturally Oriented and Integrated.** Behavioral outcomes sought from general education because the achievement of effective and desirable standards of behavior is largely dependent upon the cultural orientation and integration which enables one to participate understandingly in social, cultural, ethical, and aesthetic experiences.

1.2 Part III, pages 102 to 112

3. **Maintaining and Improving Physical and Mental Health.** Behavioral outcomes to be sought from general education because of the desirability of maintaining personal mental and physical health and of developing a healthful and safe environment.

1.3 Part III, pages 112 to 122

4. **Becoming Economically Competent.** Behavioral outcomes to be sought from general education because of the desirability of becoming economically literate and self-supporting; of making a wise choice of life work; of beginning basic common preparation for it; and of fulfilling the citizen's responsibility for safeguarding our natural and human resources.

1.4 Part III, pages 122 to 133

AREAS OF BEHAVIORAL COMPETENCE

CHART OF THE DIRECTIONS AND ARE

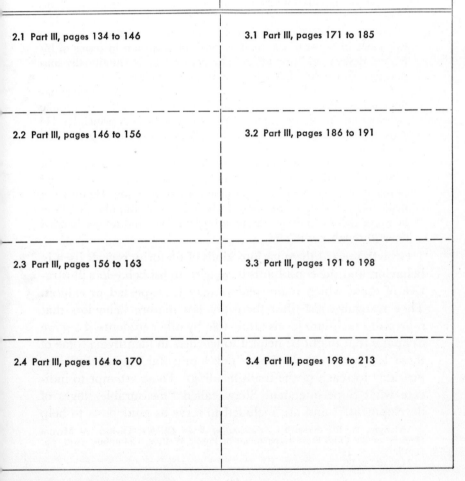

2. **Growth Toward Desirable Interpersonal Relations in Small (Face-to-Face) Groups.** General education in high school should help youth develop the common kinds of behaviors needed by them in maintaining mutually helpful and stimulating face-to-face relationships with family members, school friends, and members of community groups, and in developing the interpersonal attitudes, habits, and skills fundamental to the exercise of responsible citizenship.

3. **Growth Toward Effective Membership or Leadership in Large Organizations.** General education in high school should help youth develop the common kinds of behaviors indicative of ability to carry the responsibilities of membership or leadership in the large religious, cultural, social, political, and economic groups under whose banners the varied activities of modern man are carried on and whose successful functioning depends more upon the intelligent, effective, cooperative, and devoted services of their members than upon the intricacies of their organizational structure.

GROWTH TOWARD MATURITY

The consultants recognize that "maturity" is a composite not an integer. There are several important kinds, and the behavioral competence sought from general education may manifest itself in one or more of them. Dr. A. R. Mangus of Ohio State University has supplied a useful statement for educators when he lists and describes the following areas:

A person is socially mature when he is able to live easily, comfortably, and harmoniously with other people. The socially mature are free from neurotic necessity to dominate and control others, to be unduly submissive to them, or to withdraw from social contacts.

A person is emotionally mature when he is able to control his energies, can manage his fears, hates, resentments, and loves. The person develops in the direction of emotional maturity as he learns to live more in terms of the realities of situations than in terms of his wishes, desires, and prejudices. The person who is emotionally mature feels secure and has a healthy respect for himself.

A person is intellectually mature when he is able to size up situations and make his own decisions. He has good abilities to make decisions on the basis of known facts or on the basis of principles. He generally makes decisions with full readiness to assume responsibility for them.

A person is morally mature when he has adopted personally satisfying and socially-accepted goals of living, and when he has learned to make wise choices among possible courses of action. He does not make these choices on the basis of whim, fancy, or impulse. Nor does he make them merely on the basis of rigid rules and taboos handed down through traditions.[1]

Growth toward these various kinds of maturity reveals itself in behavior, and the consultants have tried to list behaviors illustrative of those which many seniors may be expected to exhibit. They recognize also that there are less mature behaviors that represent maximum levels attainable by other students. To serve as guides that might be helpful to teachers in identifying some of these less mature behaviors, "developmental equivalents" are provided for each of the main headings. These attempt to indicate what Superintendent Shaw called "measurable stages of development,"[2] and are included to serve as guideposts to help

[1] Mangus, A. R., *Personality Adjustment of School Children*. Division of Mental Hygiene of the Ohio State Department of Public Welfare, Columbus, 1948, pp. 17–18.
[2] *Op. cit.*, p. 86.

teachers of younger or less mature students. The ranges of individual differences being what they are, some of the developmental equivalents should be accepted as very satisfactory performance from some students. They do not represent degrees of failure to attain a goal, but stages of success which can be utilized as the basis for still further progress. It would be a mistake to assume that this study proposes that all high schools should attempt to have every student fully attain the behavioral competencies included in the lists of outcomes. But it would also have been a mistake for the consultants to have listed outcomes which did not set standards high enough to extend our most mature students toward their limits and broad enough to include examples of the various areas of maturity.

The formulation of these lists of behavioral outcomes and developmental equivalents for general education in high school is an attempt to provide worthwhile and tangible goals which will keep all students hard at work on tasks they consider important and possible of achievement. It is not a "soft" program for students, for it stresses their growth and development which result only from work on their part. As they recognize that the school is evaluating their progress by their improving behavioral competence, and their success by their willingness and ability to apply the knowledge, values, standards, and principles they acquire or learn in school, they will realize that they face tests that really challenge their ability. On the other hand, such a program of education will not present distasteful or meaningless tasks to students. The kinds of growth which it encourages them to strive for are those which they can recognize as needed by all youth if they are to lead as satisfactory and successful lives as are possible for them.

BEHAVIORAL OUTCOMES OF GENERAL EDUCATION IN HIGH SCHOOL

1. GROWING TOWARD SELF-REALIZATION.

Our democratic society has as its basic reasons for existence the protection of individuals so that they may have opportunity for full development into their best selves and the encouragement to achieve it. It is logical, then, that public secondary education in such a society should first seek to facilitate this self-realization of each student. The cultivation of willingness and ability on the part of all students to attain the kinds and levels of behavior consonant with the native endowments of each and appropriate in our kind of society and culture, therefore, should be the first concern of a high school's program of general education.

1.1   Developing Behaviors Indicative of Intellectual Self-Realization.

Behavioral outcomes to be sought from general education because the living of a satisfying personal life requires intellectual development toward the limit of one's capacity.

1.11 Improving His Study Habits, Study Skills, and Other Work Habits.

1.111 Is skillful in securing information and in organizing, evaluating, and reporting results of study and research.

Illustrative Behaviors

(a) Decides on his purpose before planning action.
(b) Practices good study and other work habits when he has intricate thinking, reading, and planning to do.
(c) Consults some good periodicals if seeking information on political developments, foreign affairs, homemaking, scientific matters, book reviews, etc.
(d) Uses common sources of printed information efficiently; e.g., dictionary, encyclopedia, almanacs, telephone directory, *Who's Who*, *Readers' Guide*, and card catalog in a library.*
(e) Can read all parts of a newspaper for needed information; e.g., weather reports, radio programs, amusements, business news, editorials, local, state, national, and international news.*

* Outcomes that were evaluated by 90 per cent of the reviewers as of "high" importance are indicated by an asterisk.

ORGANIZATION OF PROPOSED OUTCOMES

(f)   Asks questions in such a way as to secure accurate information of public services, offices, or persons likely to have special information when in need of it.

(g)   Uses books, maps, globes, charts, timetables, and graphs of all kinds to find needed information. *

(h)   Systematizes his work in order to accomplish the things he wants to do. *

(i)   Constructs line, bar, and circle graphs, diagrams, pictographs, and statistical tables to express quantitative relationships.

(j)   Uses the typewriter or writes well enough to meet his needs.

(k)   Reads and interprets the graphs, charts, tables, road, and other maps encountered in newspapers, magazines, and other popular printed matter. *

(l)   Is able to draw relevant information from several sources, correlate it, make a defensible set of conclusions, and discard what is not relevant. *

(m)   Manifests a fair knowledge of the relative reliability of various sources of information: two or more newspapers, radio and TV commentators, consumer guides, government publications. *

(n)   Develops skill in noting and recording information in outline, notes, and summary statements. *

(o)   Uses a readily acceptable footnote and bibliographical form in identifying sources of information and ideas.

(p)   Develops listening habits that enable him to gain intended meaning. *

1.112 Displays an inquiring mind: is intellectually curious and industrious.

Illustrative Behaviors

(a)   Shows by his reading, choice of TV and radio programs, attendance at lectures, and by questions, his interest in at least half of the following: economic systems and economic ideologies, international relations and foreign policy, local and national politics, local community problems, religions other than his own, social relations (relations between races, ethnic groups, social class, and economic groups), applied science, pure science, ways of behavior in various countries, art, music, history, geographic explorations, theater, movies.

(b)   Displays interest and asks questions in social groups where conversation is on topics in which he is interested and on which he is not informed.

BEHAVIORAL GOALS OF GENERAL EDUCATION

(c) Wonders about, and forms tentative opinions concerning, some matters of a philosophical nature.

(d) Perseveres and carries through industriously on an intellectual task which he has accepted.*

(e) Seeks a setting for work which is reasonably free from distractions.

(f) Recognizes need to apportion his time among the various legitimate demands made upon it, sets up a schedule of intellectual work for himself which is realistic, and holds himself to it.

(g) Follows directions intelligently.*

(h) Endeavors to have at hand the tools and materials needed for a task.

(i) Makes an effort to evaluate his practices to see whether they are consistent with his goals; attempts to determine which are the means to the ends he seeks.*

(j) Takes increasing pride in his workmanship.

1.113 Can learn independently and shows desire to do so.

Illustrative Behaviors

(a) Arranges own study plans, using school time and part of his out-of-school time.*

(b) Can set up a procedure and carry it through for a project requiring work over a period of at least a week (research report, committee projects, etc.).*

(c) Can work independently and without supervision when it is appropriate to do so.*

(d) Tries to improve his own written work by revising it so that it will convey his intention as clearly as possible.*

(e) Formulates specific and pertinent questions as a means of seeking answers on a general topic or problem on which he is working.*

(f) Adjusts his learning methods to the nature of the task; chooses between rote learning, practicing skills, using a procedure for applying general principles, etc., so as to accomplish the task.

(g) Applies what he has learned to a new situation; e.g., setting up a job on a lathe in the machine shop, applying a science principle to personal health problems, applying a principle of grammar in a foreign language, applying the method of proof he has learned in geometry to the statements made in an advertisement, etc.*

94

ORGANIZATION OF PROPOSED OUTCOMES

(h) Faces problems connected with his work realistically and attacks any task with vigor and without urging or coaxing in spite of anticipated difficulties.

(i) Criticizes himself more than others and holds himself to higher standards than he expects of others.

(j) Dares to be different when convinced that facts warrant the position.

(k) Assumes responsibility for the solution of his own problems.

(l) Is beginning to understand the nature of intellectual freedom, and the value to society and to himself of preserving the right to seek and express what one considers to be the truth.

1.114 Recognizes the importance of continuing to learn.

Illustrative Behaviors

(a) Sees learning as a continuous process throughout life.

(b) Views knowledge as exciting and worthy of further educational pursuit.

(c) Enjoys the process of learning and the development of skills, not just the finished product.

(d) Recognizes that learning occurs most effectively in terms of the individual's own effort; therefore, plans for his own growth.

(e) Looks forward to college or other type of post-high school education as a time when he can participate more fully in the culture, thus broadening and deepening his knowledge and insight.

(f) Respects scholarship for what it can do to enrich life.

Developmental Equivalents for 1.11

(Expectations for younger or less mature students)

Reads periodicals with a special interest for youth; e.g., travel, pictorials, etc.

Learning to use the dictionary and children's encyclopedias to look up the pronunciation, spelling, meaning, syllabication of words; pronunciation and identification of geographical terms and names of famous persons; meaning of foreign phrases; additional information, etc.

Obtains and uses maps, timetables, etc., when necessary.

Usually plans his work and has necessary materials before starting.

Is beginning to grasp the idea that various sources of public information are not equally valid and objective.

Is beginning to distinguish between adequate note-taking and copying information word for word.

BEHAVIORAL GOALS OF GENERAL EDUCATION

Generally needs help and encouragement in carrying through any long drawn-out or complex intellectual task.

Plans his own study program with some adult help.

Is increasingly able to take responsibility for meeting his study obligations.

Usually tries to do his best on school work and in play.

Plans for his work with increasing care and independence.

Is beginning to realize that the accomplishment of individual goals demands follow-through efforts.

Has some desire to pursue related aspects of a given topic.

Learning to make outlines with two (or even three) degrees of subordination.

Is beginning to sense the soundness of thinking before acting.

Is mindful of his own lack of knowledge and knows how to acquire ideas.

Is learning to fuse experience and theory.

Sometimes relates past experiences to new situations.

Sometimes controls himself in the face of temptation to impulsive action or statement.

1.12 Improving in His Ability to Communicate Ideas and to Recognize and Use Good Standards.

1.121 Commands and uses the basic skills of reading for information, ideas, opinions, stimulation, and leisure.

Illustrative Behaviors

(a) Adjusts his reading rate and his method of reading (skimming, taking notes for detail or for enjoyment only) to the material at hand.*

(b) Seeks consciously to attain his best reading rate and comprehension.

(c) Reads with increasing speed, comprehension, and appreciation.

(d) Makes use of newspapers, magazines, and other mass media to keep abreast of current events and to keep himself informed on important issues and developments and other matters of interest to him, but guards against the influence of propaganda, emotional appeals, bias, and prejudices.*

(e) Reads current books, magazines and journals, and the "classics" dealing with one or more special interests; e.g., science, art, drama, government, literature, music, homemaking, or biography.

96

ORGANIZATION OF PROPOSED OUTCOMES

(f)   Reads with discrimination for information or recreation books and periodicals of various types and dealing with various themes, including some of the "classics" which have influenced our intellectual climate.

(g)   Reads to find out what is happening and why; to get at the truth; to obtain directions for carrying out a project or for using new tools or equipment; and to acquire more knowledge of a field of his special interest, etc.

(h)   Reads fairly difficult and complicated writing if it deals with a particular need or interest.

(i)   Makes a deliberate effort to relate new (to him) knowledge and ideas gained from reading to what he already knows or has experienced first hand.

1.122 Expresses his ideas in speech, writing, or in some artistic form with increasing clarity and correctness.

Illustrative Behaviors

(a)   Writes and speaks with sufficient clarity and in good enough form to communicate with others.*

(b)   Organizes material which is to be presented in written or oral form into a meaningful sequence of ideas and puts them into reasonably good sentences and paragraphs.*

(c)   Spells correctly the words he uses in ordinary written discourse and uses the dictionary if uncertain of spelling.*

(d)   Seeks to find words which express his meaning accurately and which add variety and interest to the subjects about which he is writing.

(e)   Shows some individuality in expression whether it be in speaking, writing, artistic creation, or mechanical design.

(f)   Can speak before at least a small group in a pleasing manner and voice without being overcome by embarrassment or experiencing undue strain.

(g)   Accepts responsibility for correctness and honesty in his own speaking and writing: does not knowingly plagiarize.*

(h)   Writes usable outlines or summaries of important writings which he must understand and remember.

(i)   Writes social and business letters which are correct in form and clear in expression.*

97

BEHAVIORAL GOALS OF GENERAL EDUCATION

(j) Adapts his vocabulary, usage, organization, and style to his purpose and to the person or audience addressed.*

(k) Avoids overdependence upon slang, platitudinous, trite, and colloquial expressions which have no precise meaning and serve to cloud thought.

(l) Pronounces correctly and enunciates clearly the words he uses in conversation and in reading aloud.*

(m) Is trying to improve his communication skills: reading, speaking, listening, writing, or artistic creation.

(n) Practices speaking and writing another language if he recognizes this as meeting a need.

1.123 Demonstrates his command of quantitative thinking.

Illustrative Behaviors

(a) Shows some recognition of the relation of mathematics to art, music, science, social studies, modern technology, business and finance, the collection of data, the making of reports, and to the experimental process.

(b) Shows a good understanding of our number system by performing with reasonable accuracy and speed the fundamental operations with whole numbers and the major common and decimal fractions in practical problems situations; and tests the results of his computations.*

(c) Recognizes mathematics as a way of thinking and speaking about quantities, measures, amounts, sizes, and quantitative relationships.

(d) Uses when needed the common tables of weights and measures.

(e) Uses mathematics to gather data, and to present and interpret them.

(f) Demonstrates that he can read and understand mathematical reports, charts, and graphs, and simple statements of financial accounts.*

(g) Visualizes physical events accurately if he has had some experience with them.

(h) Makes logical experiments; i.e., assumes the truth of a proposition which he suspects is false, and then makes logical deductions from this proposition, as in certain proofs in demonstrative geometry.

98

ORGANIZATION OF PROPOSED OUTCOMES

1.124 Is developing some artistic and literary tastes and standards; exhibits creative capacity in some form of worthwhile intellectual activities.

Illustrative Behaviors

(a) Evaluates the results of his own activities and those of others.
(b) Respects fine performance in fields other than those of his particular interests.
(c) Has developed basic standards of color, design, and suitability in matters of dress (whether boy or girl).
(d) Takes pleasure in the beauty of his natural environment.*
(e) Distinguishes in TV and radio programs between those that are geared to superficial entertainment and those that challenge his interests in politics, art, music, social issues, and the lives of people as reflected in drama, biography, and documentaries.
(f) Visits museums—historical, fine arts, and natural history—according to individual taste in order to add to his knowledge of man's accomplishments and to increase his enjoyment of the world around him.
(g) Achieves a considerable degree of skill in one or in a few activities and seeks to become more adept in them.
(h) Seeks new ideas and procedures.
(i) Develops own standards of taste in literature, painting, and music, and can discuss his point of view.
(j) Likes to engage in reflective thinking when reflection seems called for.
(k) Displays interest in the creative work and activities of others and uses his observations to teach himself.
(l) Engages in some individual creative leisure activities: applied arts, fine arts, writing, singing, experimental activities, playing an instrument, or nature study, etc.

Developmental Equivalents for 1.12

(Expectations for younger or less mature students)
Can formulate questions to which he seeks answers, although these may often lack precision.
Is learning to take criticism.
Is gaining some skills in adjusting his reading rate to the material at hand and to his purposes in reading.
As background for many aspects of living has moderate skill in native language with reading, writing, speaking, and listening in ordinary situations.

BEHAVIORAL GOALS OF GENERAL EDUCATION

Has some skill in "unlocking" unfamiliar words.

Reads regularly at least one magazine of a quality superior to the comic book, the pulp, the confession magazine; avoids obscene and "sensational" publications.

Beginning to relate and apply material read to his present knowledge.

Improving in his ability to organize and present ideas.

Shows increasing improvement in expression, oral and written—as far as his ability will permit.

Learns common forms of correct expression.

Recognizes common geometric shapes, reads simple common fractions, dollars and cents, and numbers with four digits.

Makes simple computations without writing the numbers.

As background for many aspects of living knows enough arithmetic for the simple activities of daily life; e.g., computing the unit cost of purchases at the grocery, measuring dress goods from a sewing pattern.

Is acquiring the basic skills needed to engage in some self-expressive activity; e.g., art, music, industrial arts, dramatics.

Is growing toward personal ways of expressing himself artistically, graphically, etc.

Is beginning to exercise some discrimination in the value and use of TV and radio programs.

Listens to important public statements by government officials on radio and TV.

Shows some ability to arrive at, carry out, and defend his own point of view.

1.13 Becoming Sensitive to, and Competent in, the Use of Logical Thinking and Problem-Solving Processes.

1.131 Tends to make an objective approach to a problem and attempts to define it clearly.

Illustrative Behaviors

(a) Respects and uses with understanding the scientific method for discovering solutions to problems.*

(b) Listens to conversations and speeches effectively and understands and organizes for his own use the points made by others.

(c) Seeks for answers, asks questions, looks for causes.*

(d) Recognizes and states or defines a problem carefully and sees the necessity of doing this.*

(e) Analyzes a problem and can follow the recognized steps involved in scientific thinking.*

ORGANIZATION OF PROPOSED OUTCOMES

1.132 Seeks pertinent information and organizes and evaluates data.

Illustrative Behaviors

(a) Seeks facts, collects and evaluates information, and gathers evidence on all sides of problems which he must solve.*

(b) Shows skill in collecting data from a variety of sources and in organizing those needed to solve his problems.*

(c) Verifies data in an effort to distinguish between fact and opinion.*

(d) Evaluates evidence or authority. Recognizes stereotypes and clichés.*

(e) Recognizes bias and emotional factors in a presentation and in his own thinking.

1.133 Recognizes logical and illogical thinking in his efforts to reach reasonable conclusions.

Illustrative Behaviors

(a) Is gaining in ability to identify glaring flaws in purportedly logical discourse (e.g., circularity, *post hoc* attributions of cause, "undistributed middle") not by any particular labels but simply as unwarranted claims of proof.*

(b) Seeks to free himself from fears due to ignorance and superstitions.*

(c) Recognizes the unsoundness of drawing generalizations from insufficient evidence.*

(d) Applies generalizations to new situations.*

(e) Demonstrates some ability to reason from cause to effect.*

(f) Tries to draw logical conclusions.*

(g) Seeks to identify unstated assumptions which are necessary to a line of argument.*

(h) Recognizes that both defensible and indefensible techniques are used in attempts to influence thought and behavior: propaganda, rumors, stereotypes, emotional appeals, etc.*

BEHAVIORAL GOALS OF GENERAL EDUCATION

(i) Recognizes that accuracy and integrity are essential to critical thinking, and holds himself to the highest standards in both respects.*

(j) Views understandingly and objectively the role and significance of persuasion in our society from the standpoint of an interested consumer.

Developmental Equivalents for 1.13

(Expectations for younger or less mature students)

Sometimes tends to suspend judgment and action until after a period of deliberation.

Shows a tendency to deplore superstition, seeks causes for physical effects.

Tends to be reasonable in discussing newspaper reports of flying saucers and similar "phenomena."

Is becoming less and less gullible.

Begins to use facts to help reveal errors in what he observes, reports, reads, or hears.

Tries to distinguish between fact and rumor.

Tends to concede the force of facts even when reluctant to do so.

Improving in his willingness to accept cause-and-effect relationships as a control of his thinking and action.

Begins to gain some understanding of the scientific method and how to apply it.

Is less and less likely to make or accept too positive or sweeping statements.

Documents his statements by citing references to authorities; appreciates achievement in a given field of knowledge.

Increasingly forms opinions about his schoolmates on the basis of well-considered evidence.

Recognizes that some statements on TV and radio and in print cannot be taken at face value.

Does not too readily claim he has "proved" a point.

Is learning to recognize when statements are logical.

1.2 Developing Behaviors Indicative of Growth Toward Cultural Orientation and Integration.

Behavioral outcomes to be sought from general education because the achievement of effective and satisfactory standards of behavior is largely dependent upon the understanding of, and creative participation in, cultural, ethical, and aesthetic experiences.

ORGANIZATION OF PROPOSED OUTCOMES

1.21 **Revealing the Personal Understandings and Characteristics of the Good Citizen.**

1.211 Understands the meaning of basic democratic values.

Illustrative Behaviors

(a) Is reaching a conclusion that such democratic values as: (a) dignity of the human personality; (b) working for the good of others; and (c) utilizing the method of intelligence offer the greatest promise to man for happy and complete living.*

(b) Understands something of the origin of democratic values and man's struggle for freedom, equality, and security and begins to show his appreciation of these values.*

(c) Understands the basic characteristics of a democratic society and realizes that they are effective only as people use them as a guide for everyday living.*

(d) Understands his cultural heritage; is aware of its weaknesses but thinks they can be corrected.

(e) Recognizes the need for identifying unresolved issues in human life and shows his faith that they can be solved through the democratic process.

(f) Accepts democracy as a form of government and as a way of life.*

(g) Recognizes that freedoms, rights, and privileges demand assumption of responsibilities, duties, and obligations and begins to assume them.*

(h) Recognizes why our civil liberties are indivisible; why a denial to one person or group increasingly results in similar denials to others.*

(i) Demonstrates his belief in the importance of the development and protection of individuality.*

1.212 Practices basic democratic values.

Illustrative Behaviors

(a) Increasingly checks his own values and actions against our standards of human welfare, and the democratic traditions of freedom, the dignity of the individual, and the rights of all men.*

(b) Shows willingness to defend the orderly process and place of law, and to work actively to get change where and when needed.*

(c) Votes on all occasions when eligible and after becoming informed on the issues and candidates.*

(d) Demonstrates that he is beginning to understand the meaning and significance of "freedom with justice."*

Developmental Equivalents for 1.21

(Expectations for younger or less mature students)

Trying to understand more about the democratic way of life.

Is beginning to sense that freedoms demand responsibilities.

Begins to learn how to work for orderly change.

Learns how to vote.

Observes the customs and traditions of his society with increasing understanding.

Shows his belief in equal rights, the worth of the individual, and tolerance of differences in its early stages by his actions toward teachers and teammates, and in student government.

Avoids gang and mob action.

Discusses "justices and injustices" of events as described in newspapers; grows in his concept of rights and duties of American citizens.

Sees that all boys and girls have not lived in the same kinds of homes and communities.

Understands and defends the rights of others in specific, concrete, and simple instances.

1.22 Attaining a Perspective on Present-Day Events, Cultures, and Conditions.

1.221 Develops a sense of historical time and of cultural perspective.

Illustrative Behaviors

(a) Shows at least a general understanding of contemporary American society, the heritage which it carries, the historical roots of this heritage, and the major unsolved social problems with which it is confronted.*

(b) Has heightened perceptions of historical periods derived in part from an acquaintance with literary works of these eras.

(c) Views the world of the past as a source of insight into present-day human motivation.

(d) Recognizes the important role of national and world leaders in government, business, industry, and world affairs.*

ORGANIZATION OF PROPOSED OUTCOMES

(e) Uses our cultural past to understand the present better and as a guide to his thinking about the present.*

(f) Shows interest in learning more about world affairs.*

(g) Recognizes that within our culture there are various subcultures and appraises ideas and actions in the light of them.*

(h) Realizes that the home, the church, and the school have been, and are, institutions of fundamental importance to a democratic society.*

(i) Accepts change as a condition of living, but seeks to direct it intelligently for the benefit of himself and of society.*

(j) Is sufficiently familiar with at least the highlights of the story of the long human adventure from its origins up to the present time to give him a sense of time-relationships and to afford him some perspective on the events of his own era.*

(k) In his statements shows an understanding of the strengths and limitations of American culture (the developing culture of a relatively young country) and shows reasonableness in his evaluation of American culture in relation to the older world cultures.

(l) Appreciates the relationships between national behavior and motivating factors, such as traditional cultures, economic resources, and political conditions.

1.222 Senses the major problems and issues facing us in our relationships with other peoples in the world.

Illustrative Behaviors

(a) Appreciates by act and statement the cultures of other countries; appreciates the cultural contributions of immigrants and foreign students.*

(b) Reads about other nations to gain a better understanding of them.

(c) Understands some of the principal differences between our economic system and the economic systems of other nations.

(d) Recognizes that cultural backgrounds, physical factors, economic resources, and political conditions differ among nations and appraises ideas and action in the light of these differences.*

BEHAVIORAL GOALS OF GENERAL EDUCATION

(e) Has a growing understanding and appreciation of people whose cultures are different from his own, both those in his own community and nation and those in other areas of the world.

(f) Cultivates a strong interest in the lives of outstanding persons, past and present, of all nations and cultures.

(g) Realizes that values are related to survival. Understands that customs and traditions may operate against as well as for social intercourse.

Developmental Equivalents for 1.22

(Expectations for younger or less mature students)

Shows some appreciation of time relationships in historical and geological terms and of space relationships of the earth to the universe.

Sees the connection between some past events and conditions and some present ones.

Learns about location, geography, resources, government, and habits of people abroad.

Asks why people observe the customs they do, both in our country and in others.

Begins to accept the habits and customs of foreign students.

Reads stories about peoples of other lands.

Finds on a map distant places mentioned in the news.

Appreciates the stories of American heroes and folk heroes and tales that have their origin in the lives of the pioneer and adventurer.

1.23 Attaining Orientation to the Physical World and Appreciation of What Scientific Advancements Mean to the World.

1.231 Shows some evidence of developing an intelligent and understanding relationship between himself and the physical world.

Illustrative Behaviors

(a) Is beginning to appreciate the place of man and of the earth in the universe.

(b) Appreciates the unity and orderliness of nature.*

(c) Uses his natural environment for new knowledge, fun, leisure, recreation, and hobbies.*

(d) Visualizes the general relation of the major regions of the world to the total world map, and the United States.

ORGANIZATION OF PROPOSED OUTCOMES

(e) Knows how to secure the facts of the geography and history of the United States and to use them in intelligent discussion. Can apply knowledge of the geography and history of the world to present events and conditions in this country.*

(f) Understands in a general way the range and formation of climate and weather in the world. Secures local information about weather as needed and uses it for safe and comfortable living.

(g) Understands the effect of physical environment upon the way people live.*

1.232 Grows in ability to apply scientific fact and principle.

Illustrative Behaviors

(a) Sees the application of the basic principles of science to daily living; e.g., principles of heredity, laws of motion, activity of atoms and molecules, changes of matter and energy, origins and changes in living things, basic ideas in anthropology.

(b) Notes new developments in science—nuclear physics, electronics, plastics, photosynthesis, and the like—in popular and sometimes semi-technical publications, such as the science columns of metropolitan newspapers, *Scientific American*, the weekly news magazines, and perhaps occasionally in popular books dealing with aspects of science.

(c) Has an appreciation for a practical understanding of discoveries of science, as well as a feeling of social responsibility for their use.*

(d) Has a growing appreciation of the role of science in transforming the conditions under which men live.*

(e) Understands the relation between new scientific discoveries and national security in the modern world, and is aware of the controversy over the relative status of the United States in this respect.*

(f) Has some understanding of the materials, processes, tools, and the principal classes of manufactured products in our industrial world.

(g) Visits industries and laboratories to see science in action and to find answers to his questions.

(h) Understands the dependence of science upon mathematics, hence, of national security upon mathematics; and has some appreciation of its role in the advance of civilization.

BEHAVIORAL GOALS OF GENERAL EDUCATION

Developmental Equivalents for 1.23

(Expectations for younger or less mature students)

Shows some ability to apply scientific principles to understanding of working devices; e.g., automobile, airplane, toaster.

Begins to try to understand his physical environment.

Avails himself of many opportunities to learn more about the physical world.

As background for many aspects of living, knows enough about the physical and biological sciences to make simple applications in daily life; e.g., repairing household equipment, caring for a garden.

1.24 Improving in Ability to Apply Ethical Values as Gained from Religion, Philosophy, and Direct Experience to His Own Decisions and Behavior.

1.241 Makes an effort to relate value systems to his own and to others' conduct.

Illustrative Behaviors

(a) Expresses in his behavior a value system that places the individual human personality high, as the most precious of values; applies this system both to his own and to other people's personalities.*

(b) Has an ideal self not limited to one particular model person but made up of qualities which are mutually consistent and generally valued in our society.

(c) Modifies strong moral "beliefs" as a result of experience plus rational revision.

(d) Recognizes the claims of worthy causes on his time and ability.*

(e) Is developing an increasingly satisfying philosophy of life through study and acceptance of a system of values to guide his behavior.*

(f) Observes the customs and accepted manners—the mores—of the culture.

(g) Expresses interest in, and a thoughtful view about, problems of ethics and religion.

(h) Has a system of values in which altruism takes a high place.

(i) Demonstrates his knowledge of religious teaching and begins to develop ethical beliefs by which he wishes to live.

(j) Has established a spiritual "anchor" for himself.

ORGANIZATION OF PROPOSED OUTCOMES

1.242 Examines his own conduct and tries to improve it.

Illustrative Behaviors

(a) Recognizes his own strengths and weaknesses regarding temptations and is learning how to avoid and compensate for them.

(b) Has an excellent moral reputation in such areas as honesty, loyalty, responsibility, etc.*

(c) Demonstrates in his behavior a consistent as well as desirable value system.

(d) Uses the more commonly accepted social amenities.

(e) Is loyal to his ideals and has the courage of his convictions, but continues to examine his convictions and revise them if necessary.

(f) Guides his own conduct on the basis of a code of personal ethics and morals which he is thoughtfully working out.

(g) Tries to apply moral principles to new situations in his own life.

Developmental Equivalents for 1.24

(Expectations for younger or less mature students)

Begins to see that people think it is "right" to be guided and controlled by accepted standards and values.

Makes an effort to think about moral implications of new situations but often on very general and superficial bases.

Evidences altruism and feelings for others but not consistently, and sometimes unrealistically; accepts concept of altruism intellectually but not always emotionally.

Realizes that he ought to "volunteer" for some necessary work at home and school and acts accordingly.

Is beginning to be conscious of his value system; asks questions; tests his ideas in action; checks with the adults around him.

Shows by his actions and words that he is aware of the difference between truth and falsehood.

Begins to use ethical standards in relation to comic books, radio, and television programs and jokes.

Examines thoughtfully the popular clichés which serve to undermine ethical values: "Might makes right," "Getting the breaks depends upon whom you know, not what you are," etc.

Shows interest in, and talks about, the relationship of events (cause and effect) to certain religious tenets learned at home or church.

BEHAVIORAL GOALS OF GENERAL EDUCATION

Makes some conscious effort to formulate in his own mind ethical ideas for which he wants to strive.

Begins to state and live by the things he accepts as good or valuable.

Thinks about, and discusses on his own maturity level, ethical and moral questions as they have to do with community life and human welfare.

Is struggling to understand why society has decided some things are good, right, beautiful, and true. He is reaching for understanding in addition to knowledge.

Resists the temptation to selfishness: is willing to share.

Chooses his friends from among those whose conduct tends to conform to accepted standards.

Finds satisfaction in reading about some of the great men in history and fiction whose lives exemplify high ethical behavior.

1.25 Developing Aesthetic and Artistic Appreciations.

1.251 Shows growing enjoyment of the creative arts and participates in aesthetic and artistic activities.

Illustrative Behaviors

(a) Enjoys nature study outings; the beauty of the sea, a sunset, the forest, waving fields of grain, the stars, a storm, birds, animals, plants, etc.

(b) Pursues some individual creative leisure activities or hobbies, such as applied arts, fine arts, writing, singing, playing an instrument, nature study, cooking, sewing, costume designing, interior decoration, gardening, scientific experiments, repairing or improving a motor car, building a "hi-fi" set, collecting records, stamps, or other objects, cultivating a garden, photography, or woodworking, with growing skill and ability to evaluate the results.

1.252 Shows growing ability to appreciate and apply good standards of performance and artistic principles.

Illustrative Behaviors

(a) Has good standards of appreciation and performance in his fields of interest with which to evaluate the results of his own activities and other of others.

(b) Recognizes and applies principles of line, color, design, and functional arrangement in many situations within his sphere of influence, such as in the selection and ar-

ORGANIZATION OF PROPOSED OUTCOMES

ranging of furnishings for rooms or parts of rooms at school and at home, in the planning and arranging of food and table settings for large and small functions.

(c) Distinguishes between art objects which represent good design, line, color, and texture and those which do not.

(d) Selects color, line, and style in clothes which are attractive for him.

(e) Has a few favorite TV or radio programs of real artistic merit and attends to them regularly.

(f) Does some reading of literary merit as part of his recreation.

(g) Demonstrates definite ideas as to the essential features of a good picture, of good clothing, good architecture, good city design, good printing, and graceful dancing to appropriate rhythms.

(h) Shows growing ability to select the things he buys for their beauty as well as their usefulness.

(i) Selects for his room, or the one that serves as such, or for personal adornment, articles which meet artistic standards.

(j) Appreciates good workmanship and design in commercial products.

(k) Buys good music and works of art for pleasure.

(l) Attends musical concerts with enjoyment.

(m) Visits art exhibits with some interest and enthusiasm.

Developmental Equivalents for 1.25

(Expectations for younger or less mature students)

Is beginning to see and appreciate art, work, science, service, religion, and relationships among people.

Is developing a hobby of some kind or even a series of hobbies from stamp collecting to camp craft.

Tries out a number of creative activities from time to time.

Recognizes perspective and gets some experience in using it. Recognizes and attempts to apply standards of beauty and design in writing, drawing, etc.

Begins to show taste for good pictures, and tasteful decorations in his own room; helps decorate the schoolroom.

Listens to various kinds of music which are good of their type: dance, folk, classical, musical comedy, etc.

Exhibits some critical judgment concerning movies.

Is just beginning to get acquainted with "good" graphic art.

BEHAVIORAL GOALS OF GENERAL EDUCATION

Makes his own collection of records which may be cowboy songs, dance tunes, or real jazz.

Gaining the skills needed to make creative self-expression a satisfying experience.

Demonstrates an increasing skill in expressing dramatic experiences.

Practices developing skills in such crafts as ceramics, metalwork, leatherwork, wood- or soapcarving.

Recognizes some artistic factors in immediate surroundings.

Analyzes and evaluates his own radio listening and televiewing habits; gradually improves and balances his use of these leisure-time outlets.

At least has begun to take some interest in serious reading in one or more fields of interest.

Likes to read for pleasure.

Grows in ability to differentiate between good and cheap newsstand literature and chooses more wisely.

Tries to improve his performance in any of his fields of interest above the novice level.

Is able to make some aesthetic judgments of his own, usually in such matters as color harmony in clothes.

Recognizes some of the world's masterpieces.

Shows some appreciation of the beauty of sound, color, form, design, and arrangement encountered in daily living.

1.3   Developing Behaviors Indicative of Growth Toward Personal Mental and Physical Health.

Behavioral outcomes to be sought from general education because of the desirability of maintaining and improving one's mental and physical health and safety.

1.31 Improving in Understanding and Control of Emotional Self.

1.311 Becomes more self-reliant and independent; seeks to identify and control fears and worries.

Illustrative Behaviors

(a) Faces the consequences of his deeds and expects the same from others.

(b) Keeps himself under reasonable control as a spectator at sports contests and at other public gatherings and helps others to do likewise.

ORGANIZATION OF PROPOSED OUTCOMES

(c) Evidences sufficient personal security to withstand gang pressures to engage in activities which conflict with his own moral standards.*

(d) Is aware of the psychic needs which must be satisfied in order to have good mental and physical health—the need for response (affection, belonging), recognition, and identification (something worth-while to live for).

(e) Consciously observes peers and young adults and seeks their advice in addition to his parents' in areas of social skills.

(f) Looks inward as well as outward for causes of personal problems.

(g) Travels alone and stays away from parents with little or no homesickness.

(h) Is developing self-discipline as motivation for acceptable behavior as contrasted with dependence upon adult rules and regulations.

(i) Is learning to understand himself to the extent that he handles his own anxieties, without undue self-abuse or the abuse of others, and accepts without bitterness, physical defects, race, and other conditions which he cannot change.

(j) Evidences no prolonged moodiness or bitterness.*

(k) Does not worry continuously about physical or mental health.*

1.312 Shows increasing emotional stability.

Illustrative Behaviors

(a) Respects himself as an individual, accepting his levels of abilities and his physical characteristics (height, weight, disabilities) and adjusts his expectations of himself to them with growing grace, humor, and courage.*

(b) Is learning how to meet and deal with successes, disappointments, defeats, and frustrations with objectivity; accepting reality without undue emotional disturbance.*

(c) Shows growing understanding of the kinds of behavior which indicate unwholesome ways of meeting personal problems.

(d) Has a good sense of humor—can laugh at himself and with people, but does not laugh at them.*

113

BEHAVIORAL GOALS OF GENERAL EDUCATION

(e) Maintains an optimistic, though realistic, attitude toward life.

(f) Is proud of, but not boastful about, his accomplishments.

(g) Is eager to succeed but is realistic about his goals.*

(h) Exercises reasonable control over jealousies and rivalries.*

Developmental Equivalents for 1.31

(Expectations for younger or less mature students)

Usually takes responsibility for what he has said or done without offering an alibi.

Increasingly makes his own decisions and assumes some responsibility for the use and care of his own clothing, for his own diet, for his own recreation, and for the performance of his own school work.

Is learning how to adjust himself to other people in his immediate environment.

Is experimenting with some adult responsibilities.

Usually keeps his temper under control and does not pout or feel hurt when he does not get his own way.

Gradually comes to see that he acts poorly when he is upset or emotionally uncontrolled.

Has learned to gain some control over fear-arousing situations, such as examinations, financial problems, social situations.

Suffers mild physical injuries without emotional upset.

Is able to endure increasingly long-time lapses between expectation and fulfillment.

Is beginning to be more realistic about his goals.

Engages in active games and creative self-expression as wholesome ways of expending emotional energy and releasing aggressive impulses.

Tends toward accepting responsibilities for his own mistakes. Avoids taking refuge in rationalization or any other unwholesome mental mechanism.

Has made considerable progress in facing a normal range of tensional problems in everyday life without temper display, crying, or other extreme overt reaction, and without persisting internal strains.

Is slowly learning to relieve emotional tension in constructive ways.

Comes to terms with his handicaps without being depressed. Learns what he can and cannot do.

Is not bored with leisure; actively finds socially accepted ways to fill it; eager to learn new leisure-time activities.

ORGANIZATION OF PROPOSED OUTCOMES

1.32 Improving in Understanding and Control of Physical Self.

1.321 Views his body and its functioning objectively and scientifically.

Illustrative Behaviors

(a) Knows and takes account of the basic facts about the functioning of the human body.

(b) Manifests increasing insight concerning the growth and development of human beings and the importance of environment for such growth.*

(c) Rejects superstitions about health and illness.*

(d) Is learning to understand and to accept as a boy or girl, without undue concern and with wholesome attitudes, the feelings and normal physical phenomena accompanying sexual development.*

(e) Exhibits a wholesome interest in the opposite sex.*

(f) Distinguishes between facts and false notions and superstitutions in matters relating to sex and his own health and welfare; e.g., ideas about the relationship between masturbation and acne or venereal disease.*

(g) Seeks competent help when anxious about any sex problems or his own sex behaviors.*

(h) Is gaining an understanding of the relationship between the healthy expression of his own sex drives and his responsibility to give to his offspring a fair chance for health and happiness.*

(i) Is gaining an understanding of the spiritual as well as the physiological basis of sex and sees the relationship between the ways in which he expresses his own sex drives and the chance for health and happiness of his mate and offspring.

(j) Understands the need to distinguish between sound medical practice and quackery and tries to do so.*

(k) Uses his leisure time in a constructive manner.

(l) Takes wholesome pride in his maturing body.

(m) Realizes that the social expectations of the behavior of boys and girls, men and women are different—based upon physiological differences as well as upon patterns in the culture—and that these expectations must be critically examined for their effect upon growing personality and personality needs.

BEHAVIORAL GOALS OF GENERAL EDUCATION

(n) Has generally accurate understanding of his own strengths and weaknesses in the roles of family-member, student, worker, and friend.

(o) Appreciates the relation between developing sexual abilities and the social mores governing relationships between the sexes.*

(p) Has a good understanding of, and a wholesome attitude toward, the biology of human reproduction.*

1.322 Is learning to live and work within physical and mental health limits and to recognize signs of poor health and physical strain.

Illustrative Behaviors

(a) Recognizes the danger signals of pain, fatigue, fever, etc., exercises judgment in self-medication, and obtains medical help when necessary.*

(b) Understands and takes proper precaution to avoid contagion and sickness.*

(c) Appreciates his own mental or physical limitations or handicaps, lives with them without embarrassment or dependence on others, and avoids trying to do those things he clearly cannot accomplish.*

(d) Avoids unnecessary physical hazards and extreme exposure.

(e) Plans his living in an effort to maintain balance of physical, emotional, and social activities.

(f) Avoids leisure-time activities which contain risks of pain and dishonor; e.g., drinking, use of narcotics, sex play, fast driving, loafing on street corners.*

(g) Tries to maintain a body weight that is within the range appropriate to his age and height. (Does not undergo a rigid regimen for reducing without advice of doctor.)

Developmental Equivalents for 1.32

(Expectations for younger or less mature students)

Knows in what areas he is relatively able and effective.

Is not seriously disturbed by his own size, weight, color, and physical characteristics, physical strengths, and limitations and differences from others; usually regards his own status and his own experiences as normal; is developing a clear understanding of these differences.

Shows that he is gaining information about growth and the physiological processes.

ORGANIZATION OF PROPOSED OUTCOMES

Learns facts about health without applying everything to himself.

Knows the fallacy of common superstitions.

Discovers that much is known about our physical selves and is eager to learn more about how one grows and develops.

Learns to accept sex changes without undue embarrassment, bewilderment, or anxiety.

Is learning to distinguish between fact and superstition in matters relating to sex and his own health and welfare.

Accepts the need to correct remediable physical defects.

Begins to understand that weight is related to age and size (as influenced by heredity) as well as to growth.

Uses the correct names for the parts of the body.

Is learning about his or her sex development and recognizes that it is normal development for boys and girls.

Sees differences in people and begins to know what causes them.

1.33 Showing Intelligent Use of Accepted Health Practices, and Wise Action on Health Problems.

1.331 Is increasingly self-directive in care of his health.

Illustrative Behaviors

(a) Is well informed about, and assumes responsibility for, the care of his body; gets adequate sleep and relaxation.

(b) Can purchase, care for, prepare, and serve food which contributes to health; recognizes spoiled or unhealthfully prepared food; evaluates critically food fads; avoids dietary excesses and dissipation, and eats under conditions which discourage hurry and emotional strain.

(c) Maintains good posture and moves with increasing body-grace in walking or dancing; sits with poise and with freedom from nervous manifestations.

(d) Avoids use of narcotics, tobacco, and alcoholic beverages during the growing period and realizes the desirability of abstaining thereafter.

(e) Appreciates the relation between a sound body and a good personality and the necessity for caring for his health.

(f) Helps when necessary to eliminate insects and vermin which tend to carry germs.

(g) Selects clothing appropriate to, and enhancing, his own physical makeup, and consciously strives to become more efficient and discriminating in this respect.

BEHAVIORAL GOALS OF GENERAL EDUCATION

(h) Chooses and wears proper and becoming clothing for protection against the elements.

(i) Wears (if a girl) with growing self-assurance appropriate foundation garments and clothing properly styled for the maturing figure.

(j) Understands reasons for and enjoys physical and creative activity, seeing their relation to his physical and mental well-being and to personality and character development.

(k) Is aware that acquiring inner resources for the wholesome and enjoyable use of leisure time is to invest in character education and good mental health.

(l) Seeks to improve his skill in one or more sports or types of physical recreation.

(m) Manifests good sportsmanship at all times, either as a participant or as a spectator.*

(n) Develops the play skills and enjoys the social activities considered important by peer groups—swimming, skating, boating, social dancing, etc.

(o) Participates in some activities which involve manual skill for the pleasure he gets out of them.

(p) Pursues a hobby or enjoys an activity which requires the ability to use his hands and body—gardening, boating, model-making, hiking, etc.

(q) Initiates, or cooperates in, practices leading to the correction of physical defects; such as poor vision, poor hearing, or poor teeth. Has regular examinations.

(r) Practices habits and applies principles concerned with the control of bacteria. (Uses antiseptics and germicides for small wounds, employs methods to keep food from spoiling, safeguards milk and water supply, especially on the farm.)

1.332 Takes intelligent action on his health and hygiene problems.

Illustrative Behaviors

(a) Regularly seeks advice from medical and dental practitioners and specialists; secures medical and dental examinations, not less than once a year and more often in case of need.

(b) Uses good judgment in deciding when symptoms of illness in self or others warrant consultation with a medical adviser, and assists the doctor or dentist by defining his symptoms.

ORGANIZATION OF PROPOSED OUTCOMES

(c)   Avoids self-treatment of acne or other functional disorders common to youth.

(d)   Utilizes when necessary the health services of the community and helps others to do likewise.

(e)   Takes measures such as vaccination and immunization to protect his health and that of others from communicable disease.*

(f)   Maintains (if a girl) good habits of cleanliness, health, sanitation, and sensible exercise relating to menstruation.*

(g)   Recognizes the hazards of quack or "patent medicine" medical care and of the comparable charlatan in mental health care, and seeks to avoid these approaches to mental and physical health care.

(h)   Refuses to try a habit-forming drug and reports to the proper authority anyone offering one to him.*

(i)   Plans for adequate ventilation in all indoor situations.

(j)   Establishes habits of regularity in the elimination of bodily wastes.

(k)   Takes measures to protect himself and others when suffering from a cold or other infectious diseases.

Developmental Equivalents for 1.33

(Expectations for younger or less mature students)

Uses simple first-aid measures in dealing with minor injuries. Uses simple hygiene procedures.

Has made some effort to improve his physique and appearance.

Knows some common harmful conditions that affect health adversely — poor diet, lack of sleep, etc.

Spends much of his leisure in team-play sports but is not conscious of health benefits.

Accepts aids or devices (e.g., orthodontic braces) that will improve his physical appearance later.

Is gaining an understanding of the principles governing good eating habits and of the need for rest and physical activity.

Desires to conform to standards of dress set by own sex group, but is becoming discriminating in this respect.

Cooperates with parents by adhering to a diet if he is too thin, too fat, or has physical disorders.

Observes the principles of hygiene in the care of skin, teeth, hair, eyes, and ears, etc.

Recognizes need for some "rules" about his work, play, diet, and sleep.

Is learning to dress becomingly.

BEHAVIORAL GOALS OF GENERAL EDUCATION

Assumes good posture for his growing body.

Recognizes desirability of consulting a physician and dentist periodically.

Does not believe everything he hears about health on TV and radio, or reads in print.

Is wary of patent medicines without checking with proper authorities.

Disapproves of the misuse of drugs.

Understands the negative aspect of the use of tobacco and alcohol, and uses neither.

1.34 Making Intelligent Use of Accepted Safety Practices.

1.341 Recognizes importance of safety practices and obeys rules and regulations.

Illustrative Behaviors

(a) Knows and understands the purposes of and obeys safety laws, rules, and regulations which apply to his everyday life at home, at work, and at play.*

(b) Obeys school-building traffic regulations and helps when asked to assist in enforcing them.

(c) Has some general knowledge of accident statistics in this country and an appreciation of the costs in human life, human suffering, and economic waste which accidents cause.

(d) Understands the effects which his own physical condition, such as impaired vision, hearing, and reaction time, and fatigue may have on his personal safety and the extent to which they may make him a hazard to others; and respects the welfare of others enough not to be a hazard to them intentionally.*

(e) Removes safety hazards at home when possible and reports to proper authority safety hazards at school and in the community.*

(f) Knows where and how to report accidents, fires, etc.

(g) Observes the rules for fire-prevention in and around his home.*

(h) Exercises unusual care about fire when camping and uses the best procedures in case of fire.

(i) Obeys safety regulations around machinery and shops and in using guns, boats, fishing tackle, etc.*

ORGANIZATION OF PROPOSED OUTCOMES

1.342 Practices highway safety—as car-driver and pedestrian.

Illustrative Behaviors

(a) Has had driving instruction, passed driving test, or has qualified otherwise for a driver's license; and does not drive until he is a legal driver.*

(b) Drives a car with respect for the law and the rules of public safety.*

(c) Keeps his motor car in safe driving condition.

(d) Declines to ride in a car driven by one who has been drinking alcoholic beverages.*

(e) Demonstrates that he can observe the measures necessary for his safety as a pedestrian.*

1.343 Has first-aid skills.

Illustrative Behaviors

(a) Is able to carry out first-aid treatment following standard Red Cross procedures.*

(b) Can apply simple first-aid procedures following physical injuries (sprains, simple fractures, bleeding, etc.).

(c) Appreciates the dangers of infection and disease resulting from unattended wounds and takes proper action.*

(d) Recognizes the danger signals (odor, drowsiness, etc.) of poisonous gases.

(e) Knows rudiments of life-saving and artificial respiration; can effect rescues and resuscitation.

(f) Can swim and is competent to care for himself and others when in and on the water.

1.344 Is prepared to help meet community health and safety emergencies.

Illustrative Behaviors

(a) Knows what action has been recommended in the event of bombing, fire, or tornado at home, en route to, or in school, and acts accordingly.*

(b) Knows civil defense plans for reducing the hazards of nuclear and thermonuclear fallout following remote bomb attacks, and is prepared to help execute the plans.

(c) Knows disaster signals and directions and what to do when signals sound.*

(d) Cooperates consistently with civil safety agencies (fire, police, etc.) in regard to jaywalking, campfires, etc.

(e) Demonstrates that he knows how to call for proper emergency aid when needed.

(f) Assumes responsibility for warning younger children of potential danger and if possible removes the source of danger.*

Developmental Equivalents for 1.34

(Expectations for younger or less mature students)

Shows skills in camping (making beds, building fires, etc.), crafts, and hobbies.

Knows and obeys traffic regulations and general safety rules for automobiles.

Knows safe behavior when operating a bicycle in traffic and practices safety measures.

Is learning how to administer simple first-aid.

Realizes need and assumes responsibility for reporting accidents or crises to adult authority promptly and accurately.

Generally takes responsibility for safety of younger children where danger is obvious.

Understands and obeys the safety laws, rules, and regulations which apply to everyday life.

Is learning various measures of first-aid in school, scouts, and such agencies.

Begins to assume responsibility at school, at home, and in community for providing or maintaining safety measures.

1.4 **Developing Behaviors Indicative of Growth Toward Economic Literacy and Independence.**

Behavioral outcomes to be sought from general education because of the desirability of becoming economically literate, of making a wise choice of life-work, and of beginning basic preparation necessary for participation in any work activities.

1.41 **Preparing to Make Intelligent Choice of Life-Work.**

1.411 Surveys the world of work as a step in choosing his career.

Illustrative Behaviors

(a) Accumulates information about the many available vocations, particularly those likely to be available to him.

(b) Utilizes many resources for gaining some first-hand information about the vocations in which he might be

ORGANIZATION OF PROPOSED OUTCOMES

interested: observation of workers, visits to factories, conferences with counselors, teachers, reading, tests, films, etc.*

(c) Becomes aware of new occupational patterns and requirements emerging from such developments as electronics, automation, and the use of atomic power.

(d) Appreciates homemaking as a desirable and realistic occupational choice for girls.

(e) Learns about opportunities for education while in the armed services and takes them into account as he plans his further training and education.*

(f) Recognizes that any vocational area offers various kinds of jobs, and endeavors to become familiar with their advantages and disadvantages, working conditions, job activities, requirements for entering and for success in those which interest him.

(g) Understands that not all the work on any job can be interesting or fun, but that there is satisfaction in a day's work well done.

(h) Knows how to go about getting a job by using dependable methods and agencies.*

(i) Has had volunteer work experience related to occupational choice; e.g., as Sunday School teacher, work-experience as a teacher's aide in school if teaching is the choice.

1.412 Studies his own physical and mental capacities and interests as he surveys occupational opportunities and what they provide and demand.

Illustrative Behaviors

(a) Uses interest inventories, psychological tests, vocational interest locators, and personality inventories to help him in gaining greater self-knowledge as he chooses areas of life-work.*

(b) Shows skill in profiting by use of dependable methods of collecting information about his aptitudes, interests, and motives; and thus develops a realistic picture of his interests, abilities, and shortcomings.

(c) Has discovered in his school work some definite areas in which he is competent or superior and others in which he is less competent.

(d) If school provides program in distributive vocations, and if this is in line with his vocational goals, has taken advantage of this training.

BEHAVIORAL GOALS OF GENERAL EDUCATION

1.413 Begins to make a deliberate choice of preferred types of life-work on the basis of reason and judgment and to prepare for it in high school.

Illustrative Behaviors

(a) Has formulated some criteria for a choice of an occupation, taking into account earnings, prestige, intrinsic interest, service, security, fringe benefits, promotional opportunities, safety, health factors, etc.*

(b) Understands the objectives of the social security program, understands income tax regulations, and takes them into account as he thinks about his life-work.

(c) Is considering the selection of a worthy occupation which capitalizes his strongest vocational interests and his outstanding capacities and abilities.

(d) Is aware of: (1) the close relationship which usually exists between a parent's occupational level and the educational level achieved by his children, and (2) the close relationship usually existing between one's educational level and the occupational level which one ultimately achieves.

(e) Is following an educational plan which includes the high school courses and extra-class activities that provide the possibility of his getting the vocational and cultural values needed to enable him to develop the professional or vocational competencies required by his intended life-work.*

(f) Is doing "vocationally acceptable" work in those of his high school courses which directly relate to his chosen occupation, or work of a quality acceptable to the college or technical institution which he plans to enter.*

(g) Understands the extent to which command of the fundamental processes of communication is necessary to success in vocations in which he is especially interested.

(h) Is learning to estimate details of a job, to use the basic tools and equipment, to plan how the work should be done, and to be responsible for the quality of his own work if his choice of vocation requires these abilities.

(i) Is informed concerning the kind, length, and general cost of training for occupations and jobs in which he has an interest.

(j) Is aware of, and knows how to acquire detailed information about, the opportunities in the various branches of the armed services for prevocational training. (Mainly concerns boys.)

124

ORGANIZATION OF PROPOSED OUTCOMES

(k) Selects the college, university, trade or vocational school best suited to his needs in terms of a good education in his chosen field of work, and is preparing to meet its entrance requirements.*

(l) Is aware of the false advertising allures often used by unaccredited training schools and checks his educational plans with competent advisers.*

Developmental Equivalents for 1.41

(Expectations for younger or less mature students)

Is beginning to measure his own abilities against his vocational interests.

Eliminates from consideration those vocations for which he clearly lacks basic qualifications. (A girl with a very poor record in science should not plan to be a nurse.)

Has some knowledge of vocations and rejects earlier vocational choices which were based on childish fantasies.

Has only vague information about the income attainable from, and the prestige of, the major occupational "families."

Shows concern for knowing more about specific vocations.

Tests his abilities in an elementary way with such devices as the Kuder Test, which gives area clues but not specific vocational data.

Begins to investigate the aptitudes and requirements for various fields of work.

Thinks he might like certain kinds of work better than others.

Is interested in seeing vocational films and film strips of a general or an exploratory nature.

Learns about as many kinds of jobs as possible and requirements for success in them.

Has begun to realize that money per se—remuneration per se—is not the only reason for choosing work.

Inquires of his school counselor or other qualified persons concerning needed preparation for specific occupations.

Makes choices in the electives available to provide vocational proficiency.

Begins to narrow down his occupational interests to one or more areas, and to learn about the kind of training needed for occupations in these areas.

Is aware of some direct relationship of present training and future vocation.

BEHAVIORAL GOALS OF GENERAL EDUCATION

Knows the major groups of occupations; knows which major occupations require college education, apprenticeship, special training in school or technical institute.

Recognizes that good schooling contributes to economic success.

Knows that there are certain subjects that all who work need to have some knowledge of.

Begins as soon as possible to plan for formal education, after high school or vocational training, that is suited to his vocational interests.

Reads simple blueprints, recipes, and other types of work directions with understanding.

Learns about the work of professional or vocational organizations or unions as an aid to advancement in his career.

1.42 Becoming a More Efficient Worker Through Actual Work Experience.

1.421 Seeks actual work or other first-hand experience for practice of skills and for observation of conditions in the fields he is considering.

Illustrative Behaviors

(a) Gets some experience in working for pay during the summer.

(b) Is effective in an interview. (Makes appointment for an interview and is prompt, well-groomed, suitably dressed, and reasonably well poised.)*

(c) Fills out application forms and writes letters of application clearly and accurately.*

(d) Seeks as his placement consultants those who are well qualified and will have his interest at heart.

(e) Knows the advantages and disadvantages of using government, school, and private employment agencies, and uses them when appropriate.

(f) Notices the protections offered workers through insurance (health, accident, unemployment) which is typically carried by the employer for him.

(g) Becomes aware of the types of assistance available to workers who are forced to change jobs because of physical handicaps.

(h) Becomes more familiar with business organizations (corporate and small), labor unions, and the professional organizations as they relate to his occupational interests.

ORGANIZATION OF PROPOSED OUTCOMES

1.422 Develops good work habits and attitudes toward work and seeks to acquire desirable personal qualities.

Illustrative Behaviors

(a) Exhibits the common personal qualities and work habits needed for success in the world of work: initiative, promptness, courtesy, cooperation, cleanliness, neatness.

(b) Begins to know how to pace himself and to make a work schedule. Decides how long to work when tired; has a clear idea of time-span needed to do a job in relation to his own abilities and aptitudes and can apportion work over a week or so.

(c) Respects all kinds of socially useful work and sees the value of any work that enables man to satisfy his needs — physical, emotional, intellectual, social.*

(d) Is growing in his appreciation of the importance of ethical principles in vocational relationships.*

(e) Exhibits an appreciation of good workmanship in his special field or fields of interest.*

(f) Exhibits wholesome pride in his work or craftsmanship.*

(g) Exhibits reasonable competence in using and caring for the tools, equipment, or materials related to his emerging occupational interests.*

(h) Accepts the idea that work is a central function of human life.

(i) Develops a code of business ethics which includes a fair price, honest product, fair standards of working conditions, and fair hours of labor.

(j) Recognizes the necessity of being self-supporting or a member of a self-supporting unit.

(k) Feels responsible for making a choice of occupation.

Developmental Equivalents for 1.42

(Expectations for younger or less mature students)

Volunteers to assume responsibilities and carries them out.

Understands basic economy to the extent of beginning to understand need for saving, relationship of income to nature of employment, etc.

Tries himself out as a reliable and careful worker in the responsibilities he accepts in classroom and club activities. Tries himself out also as a reliable and careful worker in his part-time employment.

BEHAVIORAL GOALS OF GENERAL EDUCATION

Is becoming dependable in preparing a schedule and carrying it out.
Has begun to outline educational plans for the next two or three years.
Is beginning to be systematic in his work habits. (Wide variation to be expected.)
Uses fundamental vocational skills, such as reading, computation, and writing.
Accepts in good spirit reasonable compromises in the allocation of responsibilities and in the method of carrying out school jobs.
Shows by his actions that he desires to be useful and pleasant.
Has had a little experience with a few of the most common tools.

1.43 Becoming a More Intelligent and Economically Literate Consumer.

> 1.431 Recognizes importance of considering quality, price, and actual need when buying, and knows how to get reliable information.
>
> **Illustrative Behaviors**
>
> (a) Knows where to obtain accurate information about the products he wishes to buy and is persistent and skillful in using this information when making many of his purchases.
>
> (b) Makes intelligent and discriminating use of advertisements in selecting consumer products.
>
> (c) Consults labels, makes use of brand names, and reads what standardizing agencies say about competing goods before making important purchases.
>
> (d) Understands the simple economic facts of consumer economics; e.g., the factor of supply and demand, markups and discounts, charge accounts, consumers' cooperatives, stocks and bonds, effects on economy of installment buying.*
>
> (e) Exercises self-control in buying things to meet his needs and resists high pressure salesmanship.*
>
> (f) Chooses whether or not to buy mixes, precooked foods, and frozen foods, with full knowledge of what is saved or lost in preparation time and what may be lost in quality and price.
>
> (g) Takes advantage of sales, but avoids poor quality goods which are not worth even bargain prices.
>
> (h) Knows the significance of government grading of meats, dairy products, and other foods; and buys with reference to such grading.
>
> (i) Knows the major regulations of the Pure Food and Drug Act as these apply to household marketing.

ORGANIZATION OF PROPOSED OUTCOMES

(j) Checks weight and measures of the goods which he buys, and when there is a chance of error makes intelligent comparisons of food products.

(k) Acquires increasing knowledge of how to purchase and use goods and services intelligently, understanding both the values received by consumers and the economic consequences of their acts. *

1.432 Takes proper care of equipment, clothing, food, and other products for which he is responsible.

Illustrative Behaviors

(a) Keeps his possessions in adequate repair.

(b) Is able to use many common craft tools for simple operations.

(c) Uses proper methods of laundering, dry cleaning, and ironing garments made of different kinds of material.

(d) Finds out what is known about the merits of various kinds of soaps, detergents, lubricants, abrasives, etc. for cleaning and protecting household goods and equipment.

(e) Sews (if a girl) with fundamental stitches; can make a simple garment.

(f) Cleans, repairs, and stores clothing properly and otherwise tries to take good care of clothes.

(g) Employs (if a girl) the proper methods of preparing foods to preserve nutritional value and to avoid shrinkage and other forms of waste.

(h) Prepares (if a girl) palatable and attractive dishes from leftover foods.

(i) Uses proper methods of refrigeration and food storage to eliminate food spoilage. *

1.433 Is informed and competent in the handling of money.

Illustrative Behaviors

(a) Budgets his allowance or earned income to care for his immediate needs and possible emergency expenditures. *

(b) Keeps simple but accurate accounts of receipts and expenditures. *

(c) Recognizes wisdom of his family making a budget and cooperates in its effort to live within it. *

(d) Understands advantages and disadvantages to himself or family of common kinds of savings methods; i.e., interest accounts in banks and building and loan associations, Christmas Clubs, government bonds, commercial stocks and bonds.

BEHAVIORAL GOALS OF GENERAL EDUCATION

(e) Tries to save a portion of his income or allowance for a definite objective, such as a college education, ownership of a bicycle or car, travel.

(f) Appreciates the necessity for adequate insurance, and in general knows the advantages and disadvantages of each type for him or his family.

(g) Reads about and studies various kinds of insurance, including life, health, auto, and property, as a way of developing criteria by which to determine the ingredients of a good insurance program.

(h) Understands the danger in adopting an insurance plan which he cannot sustain or which denies him or his family legitimate enjoyments.

(i) Gets expert and impartial advice before selecting annuity and life insurance plans in accordance with present or anticipated need.

(j) Knows how to obtain reliable information on appropriate and adequate budget allotments for incomes and families of varying size.

(k) Knows how to draw and endorse checks properly for his own protection.

(l) Knows how to use a personal checkbook as a way of keeping an accurate account of expenditures.

(m) Avoids carrying on his person, or keeping in the home, large sums of money.

(n) Knows the protection afforded by money orders, traveler's checks, registered mail, and postal insurance,

(o) Is informed about various sources from which to borrow money (banks, credit unions, installment buying, personal insurance, real estate mortgage); can figure the interest he or his family is asked to pay, and compares the relative advantages of these methods for a particular purpose. *

(p) Understands the reason interest is charged.

(q) Understands why his family pays taxes, and knows in general what taxes are paid and what is received in return. *

(r) Understands the basic features of the Social Security Act and the benefits which he or his family can eventually gain. *

Developmental Equivalents for 1.43

(Expectations for younger or less mature students)

Likes to earn a little money of his own.

Feels responsible for eventually getting and holding a job.

ORGANIZATION OF PROPOSED OUTCOMES

Has some knowledge of the simple economic facts of consumer economics; e.g., law of supply and demand, markups and discounts, charge accounts, consumers' cooperatives.

Accepts a share of responsibility for the family marketing in order to gain experience in buying with reference to government grading practices.

Discounts extravagant claims of advertisers.

Has some awareness of consumer guide literature.

Compares installment buying with buying for cash and develops skill in computing interest rates charged in installment buying.

Understands about taxes in general.

Knows of the existence of the common kinds of savings methods, but does not have a clear understanding of each.

Knows a little about the general types of insurance.

Gains experience in planning his expenditures with reference to his major needs and to the amount of his allowance or his earnings from part-time jobs.

Generally spends money when he gets it, but is beginning to plan on making purchases which will require him to save money.

Learns about personal budgets.

Learns about the nature and purposes of banks.

Knows about checking accounts, but has no understanding of their operation.

Shows interest in why parents carry life insurance.

Learns how to make out an income tax return.

Has experienced the need for saving to meet some unexpected situations.

Recognizes earning, saving, and spending as immediate personal problems.

1.44 **Manifesting Intelligent Understanding of Our National Economic Life and Institutions.**

1.441 Recognizes the free enterprise system as a dominant factor in American economic life.

Illustrative Behaviors

(a) Has general knowledge of the meaning and importance of capitalistic financing of business in America, of the relations of government and business, and of the interest of the general public in the financing and operation of our free enterprise system.

(b) Recognizes in a general way the uses and abuses of the American profit system.*

131

BEHAVIORAL GOALS OF GENERAL EDUCATION

(c) Is able to compare and contrast major aspects of the different ways of organizing economic life, such as capitalism, communism, fascism, and socialism.

(d) Understands in a general way how prices and wages are set and profits determined.

(e) Recognizes what has happened to major economic areas (agriculture, industry, etc.) because of advances in technology and research.

(f) Demonstrates his ability to understand the importance of large pressure groups (business, veterans, farmers, labor) in national politics.

(g) Appreciates to some extent the relations between population, resources, technology, stable employment, trained manpower, national peace, free labor, and economic prosperity.

(h) Appreciates the value of experimental activities and research related to various aspects of the economy (agriculture, commerce, consumers, etc.).

(i) Appreciates the relations between economic prosperity, adequate incomes for all, and a high standard of living.

(j) Begins to understand the relation between income, consumer spending, and a balanced economy.

(k) Appreciates the need for new markets abroad, new products, new local demands, more earnings widely distributed to increase production; and the necessity for allowing foreign products to be sold in this country.

(l) Is familiar in general with the productive and distributive system for goods and services.

(m) Recognizes importance and problems of good labor-management relations.

(n) Is familiar in general with our monetary system and banking.

1.442 Recognizes need for taking personal interest in, and responsibility for, conservation of natural resources.

Illustrative Behaviors

(a) Studies current problems of production, consumption, and distribution of natural resources as a way of becoming more intelligently participative in the work-life of the world.

(b) Obeys laws and rules made to conserve natural resources, fire-prevention, reforestation, preservation of wildlife, land, conservation, etc.*

ORGANIZATION OF PROPOSED OUTCOMES

(c) Is careful and economical in his use of materials—clothing, food, school and home equipment, books and school supplies.*

(d) Forms tentative judgments as to how society can fulfill its responsibility for conserving human and material resources.

(e) Understands the issues involved in the wise and intelligent development of natural resources.*

Developmental Equivalents for 1.44

(Expectations for younger or less mature students)

Begins to understand reasons for change in employment, change in security status; e.g., changes in child labor laws, changes in father's employment.

Learns about the nature and purposes of banks.

Learns the differences in standards of living in different groups and regions.

Reviews a number of new inventions of recent years which have been important.

Learns something about stocks and bonds, big business, little business, and partnerships.

Learns about mechanization and the changes in life on the farm and in production during the past twenty-five years.

Learns about the work of the Department of Agriculture and other such governmental agencies.

Studies the new factories in his community, the things available now that were not available a few years ago.

Learns something about the ways in which our American economy works; studies resources, transportation, communication, factories.

Is learning how various goods are produced, distributed, and conserved.

Is becoming acquainted with our natural resources and is learning how they serve people.

Recognizes that he should not be destructive of various goods and materials even if he is not always careful.

Is beginning to feel that nothing should be wasted.

Helps to care for and protect public property.

Obeys regulations concerning the use of recreational facilities.

2. **GROWING IN ABILITY TO MAINTAIN DESIRABLE SMALL (FACE-TO-FACE) GROUP RELATIONSHIPS.**

The richer and more satisfying life which general education in high school seeks to enable youth to enjoy is partly dependent upon the mutually helpful and stimulating face-to-face relationships one is able to develop and sustain between himself and others in his family, in his school, in his neighborhood, and in social peer groups of boys and girls. Growth and development toward responsible citizenship in a democratically oriented society, a correlative purpose of general education, has its foundations in the attitudes, habits, and skills which must first be acquired by children and youth in their face-to-face group relationships.

2.1 Developing Behaviors Indicative of Intellectual Growth and Development.

Behavioral outcomes to be sought from general education because the advantages of small group membership depend in part upon one's ability to join in, to contribute to, and to enjoy the intellectual interests and activities of such groups.

2.11 Manifesting Acceptable Family Membership.

2.111 Maintains understanding relationships with parents and other family members.

Illustrative Behaviors

(a) Understands that families have different ways of meeting their needs; that there are many variations in family customs and patterns of living and that these are learned from the subculture to which the family belongs.

(b) Enjoys reading aloud on occasion from good books or periodicals to other members of the family, or listening to others read aloud.

(c) Takes pride in family traditions and customs which bind the family together and give pleasure to its members.

(d) Growing in ability to respect the rights, possessions, and privacy of his brothers and sisters and parents and to share fairly common family possessions.

(e) Appreciates the differences that exist in members of a family, in interests, taste, desires, and goals; and shows growing insight into how to develop relations which contribute to a well-balanced home life.

(f) Is usually thoughtful of his parents and does not make unreasonable demands on their time or financial resources.

(g) Shows evidence of understanding of self in relation to his family—to its background, present-day living practices, ideals, and concern for the future.*

(h) Understands and tries to channel his emotions in relation to the family and others.

134

ORGANIZATION OF PROPOSED OUTCOMES

(i) Appreciates that children at various maturity levels have their own ranges of accepted behaviors; knows individuals mature at different rates—mentally, emotionally, and socially—and, therefore, he is more understanding of them. *

(j) Understands that living democratically at home involves sharing and self-discipline. *

(k) Knows where to go for knowledge which he can use to help solve family problems and where to go for additional preparation for homemaking and parenthood. *

(l) Tries to understand the meaning of, and to exemplify, ethical and moral virtues in the give-and-take of family life. *

(m) Is striving to identify concrete values of family living so that he may enjoy them in the family in which he is living and to preserve them in the family he will establish. *

(n) Recognizes that a growing independence of family is a natural part of growing up, but makes a realistic evaluation of parents' expectations and viewpoints, and is usually thoughtful of parents. *

(o) Realizes that there is a reason why members of a family behave as they do; that it is important to look for the reason. *

2.112 Participates in family activities and does his share of work around the home.

Illustrative Behaviors

(a) Interested in younger brothers and sisters, helps them with their problems; acts as adviser and friend.

(b) Shares selection of radio and television programs with members of the family.

(c) Understands that happy and harmonious family life means participation of all members in the work and enjoyment of the home and assumes his share of the responsibilities without thinking that he is being imposed upon. *

(d) Participates in and appreciates the kind of family planning which recognizes the interests and need for independence of each member, yet provides help and strength for all. *

(e) Enjoys participating in discussions of currently important and interesting matters with other members of his family, and utilizes information and understanding gained from his school experiences in contributing to discussions in the home.

BEHAVIORAL GOALS OF GENERAL EDUCATION

(f) Is interested in engaging in one or more intellectual activities or hobbies with his family.

(g) Recognizes that vacation trips with his family are opportunities for enjoying and learning about nature and the world about him, and for enjoying family relationships without the usual stresses of everyday living.

(h) Begins to appreciate his family as the testing ground of ideas, values, and problems; and solicits honest reactions.

2.113 Is beginning to anticipate the possibility of having a home of his own some day.

Illustrative Behaviors

(a) Is familiar with his proper role in dating and the common courtesies of dating; manifests some understanding of the desires and differences of the opposite sex, and is able to enjoy a wide range of wholesome activities with them.*

(b) Understands the role of sex in personality development, its importance in dating, and its place in courtship and marriage.

(c) Gives thought to what his home will be like, what his marriage partner will be like, and the importance of preparation for marriage.

(d) Is realistic in looking toward marriage.

(e) Recognizes that problem situations in marriage require adjustment on the part of both marriage partners.

(f) Understands the importance of choosing a marriage partner wisely.*

(g) Begins to appreciate the importance of being sensitive to the personal feelings and desires of the opposite sex.

(h) Begins to understand the importance of shared interests and mutual respect and consideration in marital happiness and in security with his mate.

(i) Applies his own code of responsible or ethical behavior without being prudish or unacceptable, but with firmness and poise.*

(j) Understands and accepts the regulations and restrictions placed by social mores upon sexual expression.*

(k) Recognizes that differences in family background, personality patterns, religion, education, and social status play a part in ability to make adjustments in marriage.*

(l) Knows something of the legal aspects and obligations of marriage.

(m) Has some understanding of the chief causes of divorce; recognizes that failure in marriage is usually the fault of both parties and that both may need the help of a marriage counselor or psychologist.

(n) Knows the services available for marriage counseling in the community and how to use them if and when needed.

(o) Appreciates the meaning of sharing, love, and companionship, the different interests and needs to be met by mates and children.

(p) Recognizes the importance of medical examinations and care of the prospective mother during pregnancy.

(q) Understands the place of children in a family and the obligations of parenthood.*

(r) Knows at least some sources of information and guidance in child care and training and how to use them.

(s) Understands the effect of love and security upon the personality of children, and that a happy, secure childhood contributes strongly to happy, well-adjusted adult life.*

(t) Understands something of the growth characteristics and needs of children, and the common health problems of childhood and how to care for them.

Developmental Equivalents for 2.11

(Expectations for younger or less mature students)

Is becoming more aware of himself as a member of his family—of his individual role in the family life and of his family responsibilities.

Is interested in understanding self in relation to parents and his peers.

Learns how to care for brothers and sisters and to "baby sit."

Shows respect for parents and grandparents and family friends.

2.12 Sustaining Friendly Contacts with One's Friends and with Others in Small Unorganized Groups.

2.121 Has friendly attitudes toward others and ability to accept them as individuals.

Illustrative Behaviors

(a) Learning to meet adults with ease and gets along with age-mates of both sexes.*

(b) Selects friends with discrimination.

(c) Is developing a clear idea of his most acceptable self and is learning to make the most of his personal assets.

BEHAVIORAL GOALS OF GENERAL EDUCATION

(d) Enjoys friendships and shows that he knows the qualities necessary for developing friendships. (He is loyal, just, fair, trustworthy, and keeps confidences.)*

(e) Is tolerant of the mistakes of others; offers assistance generously; inquires about the work, health, and activities of his associates, encouraging them to develop themselves through participation in group-activities.*

(f) Does his "good turns" unobtrusively and spontaneously, and is willing to make sacrifices for others.

(g) Shows that he can be congenial on group dates, manifesting his best personality without undue demonstration.

(h) Is sensitive to the feelings of others, helping those who are weaker or younger than he is.*

2.122 Is developing character qualities and command of social courtesies and skills needed in interpersonal relationships.

Illustrative Behaviors

(a) Avoids disagreeable habits (filing or cleaning nails, "snapping" knuckles, picking teeth in public), and grows in his ability to evaluate his own behavior by high standards of conduct.

(b) Shows by word and deed that he recognizes the importance of high standards of behavior and of their importance for personal respect and a stable society.

(c) Is successfully establishing acquaintances with others of his own age, and finding joy in many wholesome activities with them.

(d) Is gaining confidence in his ability to win the friendship and respect of members of the opposite sex.*

(e) Manifests by his actions his stand against snobbery, and other expressions of inferiority and superiority in social relationships.

(f) Uses the etiquette needed to handle the range of common social situations in which he is involved.*

(g) Knows the mores and standards of his social groups, the reasons for them, and the consequences of violating them.

(h) Is skillful in putting others at ease and in making them feel wanted in the group.*

(i) Shows that he can be an individual without being stubborn or unkind, and is willing to modify personal preferences in favor of those of others.*

ORGANIZATION OF PROPOSED OUTCOMES

(j) Apologizes for errors and blunders and injury to others with speed, ease, and sincerity.*

(k) In discussions on controversial matters concedes as much as possible to the position of one who disagrees and expresses disagreements.

(l) Makes every effort to resolve conflicts; is willing to compromise and yet is sensitive to principles, errors, and differences.

(m) Leads others to share opinions with him without domination.*

(n) Acquires insight into "human nature" (behavior), so that in his dealings with others he is able to accept their foibles with some humor and tolerance.

(o) Begins to set his own standards and values, in harmony with the best he knows, accepting or rejecting for himself ideas and conduct in terms of his own developing theory of living.

(p) Knows the rules and is somewhat skilled in several of the games, sports, and other group activities of his own sex or of both sexes, and is skilled in some of them.

(q) Recognizes the value of group association to develop ease and poise and to widen and deepen his interests.

2.123 Improving in his ability to communicate in conversation with, and in writing to, another (personal letters— furnishing information or giving directions).

Illustrative Behaviors

(a) Expresses himself orally in language that is clear, simple, effective, and appropriate to the group situation in which he is participating.*

(b) Guards against snobbery toward those whose speech patterns differ from his own.

(c) Adapts his language, including his selection of anecdotes, to the nature of the group or the individuals with whom he is conversing, but avoids vulgarity, profanity, and bad taste in conversations.

(d) Possesses a fund of information and reacts to situations which enable him to help in carrying on a good conversation without attempting to dominate it.*

(e) Helps to maintain a thoughtful level in conversation, although he does not always insist upon talking about serious matters.

(f) In conversation, refers to books he has read and would like to read when it can be done without seeming to be "showing off."

(g) In social gatherings generally avoids topics which may lead to unfriendliness.

(h) Is developing the ability to recognize disjunctions and incompatibilities among statements and events and to identify glaring flaws in what is supposed to be logical discourse. *

(i) Corresponds with friends and others through letters and other forms of written communication.

(j) Observes adequate form in business letters.

(k) Employs language in his writing that is clear and simple; punctuates his sentences in such a way as to facilitate ease of reading; spells correctly; and avoids the major errors in grammar.

Developmental Equivalents for 2.12

(Expectations for younger or less mature students)

Is learning to accept others.

Recognizes that all do not hold same beliefs or patterns of behaviors.

Begins to appreciate and try his abilities in the various creative means of expression, such as the arts, languages, crafts, good workmanship, and the various forms of written communication.

Is beginning to develop good social manners appropriate to the occasion.

Is learning to discriminate in selecting and keeping friends.

Is increasingly at ease in a mixed social group.

In his conduct with others shows greater loyalty and courtesy.

Makes introductions properly and more easily.

Observes rules of courtesy in making and receiving telephone calls, and does not monopolize a telephone line.

Learns the reasons for differences in people—talent, ability, cultural background.

Is developing good manners for his own range of experience.

Is growing in friendliness toward others, with increasing understanding of the qualities essential in friendship.

Avoids trying to impress others.

Expresses ideas clearly so that his contemporaries as well as his elders will understand.

Writes an interesting and informative letter to a member of the family or to a friend about what he has been doing or activities at home or in school.

ORGANIZATION OF PROPOSED OUTCOMES

Learns to do things for others and to overcome his own selfish desires. Is beginning to get satisfaction in rendering services that contribute to the welfare of others, not merely to himself. Is sensitive to the feelings of others. Differs in opinion on occasion from his fellows and accepts such behavior in others. Gains more confidence by increasing his knowledge and his success.

2.13 Developing Behaviors Indicative of the Kinds of Competence Needed as a Member of Small Organized Groups.

2.131 Joins organized groups when their purposes relate to his tastes and interests, and develops the personal characteristics which contribute to successful small group membership.

Illustrative Behaviors

(a) Is actively identifying himself with organizations or groups with intellectual, cultural, or social service interests as well as those with purely social interests.

(b) Uses good judgment in the number of groups he joins, so that his interest will not be too widely dissipated and his contributions, therefore, limited.

(c) Participates with others in organizing school activities outside the classroom, and contributes or supports worthwhile proposals. Registers his disapproval of proposals which seem unacceptable to him.

(d) Shows the understanding and skill necessary to participate effectively in the affairs of an organized group; becomes a participant in school government; attends school functions and can discharge the duties of office or committee membership if called upon.

(e) Sees in club activities opportunities for the growth of the members.

(f) Cooperates with others from a sense of feeling the unity of group endeavor, but knows when to work alone.*

(g) Is able to raise important questions and to present information and his own experiences which provide new insights and information into the problems under consideration.*

(h) Is developing appropriate standards by which to appreciate and evaluate his performance and that of others in a group.

BEHAVIORAL GOALS OF GENERAL EDUCATION

(i)   Cooperates with others in setting up acceptable purposes and plans for judging the success of school activities and for building a standard of behavior for school
affairs.*

(j)   Is able to devise ways to relate the activities of the school
to the activities of other agencies in the community for
recreation, leisure interests, and character building.

2.132 Helps to plan group activities and does his share in carrying out plans.

Illustrative Behaviors

(a)   Accepts and discharges responsibility for helping to define goals for a group's work and for finding satisfactory
procedures to achieve them.*

(b)   Helps to plan group work and carries his share of responsibility in working out these plans in such a manner
that the enjoyment of the group is enhanced and its
efficient operation promoted.*

(c)   Shows insight in appraising the area in which he and
other members of a club or class can make their best
contribution and encourages an appropriate contribution from each.

(d)   Thinks critically with reference to problems affecting
the group life of the classroom or club.*

(e)   Knows how to find appropriate program materials to
use with his club, group, or class.

(f)   Seeks to become informed, and contributes information,
on the issues presented to organizations to which he belongs; listens to other points of view; and asks questions
to clarify points or to further the discussion.

(g)   Contributes any special abilities he may have (initiating
art projects, serving on a poster-committee, organizing
and directing small musical or dramatic groups, selecting appropriate music for programs, and even accepting
responsibility for drudgery and routine tasks) and volunteers occasionally for such assignments and responsibilities.

(h)   Is completely reliable in handling the finances and
property of a club or class.*

(i)   Takes his full share in student government activities,
assists in selecting student officers, is willing to run for
office, or to support others, votes in school elections.*

ORGANIZATION OF PROPOSED OUTCOMES

2.133 Works well with others while maintaining his own views, ideas, and standards.

Illustrative Behaviors

(a) Works cooperatively with other members of the groups to which he belongs and strives for good human relations in the group.*

(b) Is able to act as host or hostess for a group gathering.

(c) Endeavors to be prompt in his responsibilities to the group.*

(d) Demonstrates good team play by submerging his own role into one which is for the good of the team.*

(e) Appreciates the importance of a feeling of kindred interests and of the power of group action.*

(f) Understands and appreciates the value of teamwork in the solving of many intellectual problems and recognizes the possibility of giving and gaining intellectual enrichment through this pooling process.*

(g) Respects the rights and decisions of others in group work.*

(h) Can state clearly an individual or minority opinion in group planning and can clarify the basis for his position.*

(i) Tries to apply facts, data, and principles, and considers consequences in making his decisions.*

(j) Will stand up against group leaders if he thinks they are in the wrong.*

(k) Helps the groups of which he is a member isolate and deal logically with the issues under discussion and to discuss them objectively without derogatory personal references.*

(l) Identifies and evaluates many of the values he is using in judging a projected course of action.*

(m) Is developing ability to recognize the need for evidence leading toward acceptance or rejection of a generalization and is strengthening the disposition to look for it.

(n) Is developing the ability and the disposition to formulate explanatory hypotheses on recognition of disjunctions in his experiences.

(o) Often identifies unstated assumptions which are necessary to a line of argument and has the disposition to look for them.

BEHAVIORAL GOALS OF GENERAL EDUCATION

(p) Has the ability to recognize vagueness or ambiguity and the skills for dealing with either in serious discourse.

(q) Will argue in support of a proposal on which he has deep convictions even though he knows the majority of the group oppose it.

(r) Is sympathetic in his recognition of the values and value systems of others. *

2.134 Uses democratic values and practices in organized group activities and in relations with fellow members.

Illustrative Behaviors

(a) Uses his background of knowledge and understanding of democracy in participating in organized school-group activities (student government, club, and class affairs). *

(b) Manifests in his own behavior such democratic qualities of personality as cooperativeness, personal responsibility, concern for others, and open-mindedness and consideration for the value systems of others. *

(c) Is increasingly able to find ways to deal constructively with disagreements when they arise in a group; and is concerned to protect the rights of any minority group when there is a difference of opinion in the group, especially when the minority opinion is not his own. *

(d) Can accept group decisions and work for their fulfillment even though he may not agree wholeheartedly, unless he has a deep conviction that the group decision is inconsistent with his developing ethical principles or moral judgments. *

(e) Avoids unfair delaying tactics as a means of thwarting the will of the majority but recognizes desirability of delay if there is need for more information or if a wide divergence of opinion exists.

(f) Knows the reason for the secret ballot and insists upon its use in elections or in other matters where individuals must feel free from outside pressures.

(g) Resents substitutes for democracy (machine tactics, dictatorial leaders) and opposes such practices by speech and action.

(h) Takes an active part in supporting the progressive enlargement of the sphere of student participation in the government of his school in cooperation with school authorities.

ORGANIZATION OF PROPOSED OUTCOMES

(i) Presides or acts as chairman of a small group when asked to do so, and plans carefully for group undertakings when he is in charge. *

(j) Makes his choice of officers or leaders on the basis of their fitness and qualifications for the office or the responsibility. *

(k) As leader or participant in a group, tries to see that democratic standards are adhered to. *

Developmental Equivalents for 2.13

(Expectations for younger or less mature students)

Is learning to recognize and to play certain expected roles in society and to accept, at least for consideration, standards set for him.

Practices leadership and group discussion.

Interrupts infrequently and quietly, and only when this may clarify and advance the discussion.

Participates in wide range of activities suitable for his age and learns the social amenities for various occasions.

Will assist, if called upon, in preparing for parties and social functions.

Learns to secure facts and data before making decisions.

Begins to appreciate excellence in performance.

Is beginning to feel secure enough in his group relationships to examine right and wrong courses of group-action.

In homeroom advisory group, service groups, and councils, cooperates intelligently in solving problems of the school community.

Participates actively and thoughtfully, with growing awareness of his responsibilities in a democratic group.

Compares folkways, customs, aesthetic and social values among communities in a broad and general way.

Is learning the technique of research so as to be informed on issues to come before his group.

Learns about the teachings of religious groups and the activities of church groups.

In group work, expresses his point of view, listens to others; modifies his previous point of view where merited as a result of the discussion; is beginning to help resolve conflicts in group discussions.

Practices social courtesies as a speaker and listener.

Is learning about the history and important events in the community from the actual participants.

Helps with programs, social affairs, clean up, invitations, etc.

BEHAVIORAL GOALS OF GENERAL EDUCATION

Feels himself a member of a group which undertakes to solve a community problem and gets personal satisfaction from the success of his group.

Participates in such organizations as Future Farmers, 4-H Clubs, Model Unions, junior businessmen, future teachers, or junior achievement groups.

Is beginning to distinguish an appeal based on reason from one based on emotions.

Begins to recognize that there is a relationship between his actions as an adolescent and the kind of citizen he will be as an adult, and is trying to put into practice behaviors which he considers important.

Is beginning to accept the decisions of the group graciously after he has had an opportunity to say what he thinks.

Is willing and able to give recognition to others for their contribution to group activities.

Takes responsibility as a group member and officer; chooses group leaders on their merits for an assignment.

Begins to understand and participate in the process of group action.

2.2   Developing Behaviors in Small Group Situations Indicative of Cultural Orientation and Integration.

Behavioral outcomes to be sought from general education because the advantages of small group membership depend in part upon one's ability to appreciate, to understand, and to participate in cultural, ethical, and aesthetic interests and activities of such groups.

2.21 **Improving Understandings and Attitudes Which Facilitate Desirable Relationships Within the Family.**

2.211 Recognizes importance of the family as a social institution.

Illustrative Behaviors

(a)   Recognizes and appreciates the importance of the role of the family in society.*

(b)   Understands something of the changing role of the family in American culture and the problems faced by modern families due to social changes.*

146

ORGANIZATION OF PROPOSED OUTCOMES

   (c)   Understands in a general way the basic facts of heredity and eugenics. *

   (d)   Understands the biological function of the family.

   (e)   Notes and begins to have an understanding tolerance oɪ the differences in customs respecting food habits, dress, manners, and discipline of children among families of different religious, national, and socioeconomic backgrounds.

2.212 Appreciates opportunities for cultural and intellectual activities within the family.

Illustrative Behaviors

   (a)   Has the ability to entertain other members of his family and friends in ways consistent with the resources available and his family situation.

   (b)   Cooperates in the gradual building of a well-chosen home library.

   (c)   Discovers books and magazines articles on subjects of interest to members of the family and calls them to their attention.

   (d)   Takes pride in the good appearance of his home, neighborhood, and community. *

   (e)   Is interested in taking part in discussions of, and helps in work concerned with, beautifying the home.

   (f)   Understands the purpose of zoning laws and supports them.

   (g)   Seeks increasing opportunity for expanding his creative activities with the family group. *

Developmental Equivalents for 2.21

(Expectations for younger or less mature students)

Has a growing appreciation of the importance of the family in society.

Is growing in understanding of each member's responsibility in family plans and projects, and in a desire to consider the wishes and needs of other members of the family.

Is eager to achieve some independence of the family and is beginning to find ways of doing so that gain family approval.

Is interested in understanding why younger children sometimes seem to be "pests."

Enjoys participating with other family members in some type of creative activities in the home.

BEHAVIORAL GOALS OF GENERAL EDUCATION

Shows appreciation of some art standards by the choices he makes in everyday life.

Is beginning to sense that the family is a good laboratory for learning how to get along with other people and how to carry a share of the responsibility in group activities.

Is beginning to realize how his own feelings can affect his relationships with others in the home.

Is gaining an understanding of his parents' points of view—their anxiety about their children's safety and their need to feel important in the lives of their children.

Recognizes the motives for his family's interest in his education, vocation, social life, recreation, religion, but knows he should be able to make his own decisions.

Is interested in seeking background for understanding conflicts with and among family members; tries to refrain from aggravating situations.

Is beginning to realize that conflict with his parents or other adults in such matters as his appearance—dressing like the crowd—and how he spends his time and money is normal.

Counsels with his parents but begins to develop his own judgment and good reasons for his actions.

Recognizes his own need to feel on his own in many situations, but also that it is normal to want to return to "home base" for security and understanding.

Is developing some successful action patterns in terms of increasing independence, as for example, in making decisions and assuming responsibility for use and care of his own clothing, for his own recreation, and his own diet. Realizes that parents are more likely to allow one to make choices when he has proved he can make them wisely.

Is beginning to understand that his own behavior has an effect on the attitudes and behavior of other members of his family.

Sees his natural resistance to adult domination as a part of his growth toward maturity.

Shows a healthy interest in younger children.

Has learned that helping the family can be satisfying.

Is becoming aware of adult responsibilities in marriage and family life, and that in today's changing world special preparation for these responsibilities is needed.

Is learning to understand money management problems involved in maintaining certain aspects of the home.

Keeps his parents reasonably aware of his activities and intentions.

When taking care of younger sisters or brothers, entertains them with discrimination; e.g., selects better music, stories, etc.

ORGANIZATION OF PROPOSED OUTCOMES

2.22 Adopting Cultural and Social Amenities Required in Contacts with Friends and Others in Small Unorganized Groups, and Desirable Interpersonal Attitudes and Skills in Processes Needed in Such Groups.

2.221 Displays in serious, but informal, small group discussions, the interests, knowledge, and techniques needed for acceptable participation.

Illustrative Behaviors

(a) Is able to discuss current issues and topics of national, local, or personal interest with friends and acquaintances.*

(b) Attends lectures or group discussions beyond the demands of his school work.

(c) Listens to others in conversation and discussion with a genuine effort to understand their point of view or their meaning.*

(d) Is slow to reject the ideas of others until he has examined them in the light of available facts.*

(e) Is responsive to the opinions of others, but is able to defend his own point of view.*

(f) Is learning to understand and analyze the beliefs and behaviors of others rationally, and to accept them as objective facts even though he may disapprove of them or they are not consistent with his cultural or social background.*

(g) Generally checks the facts and feelings involved in communication with others.*

(h) Supplies, when possible, reliable information to clarify a point in discussion.*

(i) Enjoys associating with people for the cultural and aesthetic enrichment they offer him.*

(j) Enjoys participating with others in a variety of intellectual activities, such as listening to them discuss books they have read; listening to record collections; attending plays and concerts and discussing them afterward; commenting on TV performances; observing and commenting upon natural phenomena and learning about the hobbies of others.

149

BEHAVIORAL GOALS OF GENERAL EDUCATION

2.222 Uses organized group activities as a means of developing artistic, creative, social, and political interests and abilities.

Illustrative Behaviors

(a) Participates in small group discussions with effectiveness and with respect for differences of others.*

(b) Makes accurate reports on classroom activities or reports to the group as a representative of it.

(c) If he gives informal talks to groups, he gives careful consideration in the selection of his material to the probable interests of his audience.

(d) Utilizes the various media of expression in arts, crafts, language, etc., to communicate effectively in a group.

(e) Participates in activities of creative groups according to his interest—demonstrates or performs effectively before small groups (music, art, industrial arts, dramatics).

(f) Appreciates and understands the different cultural, political, racial customs, beliefs, and heritage of other members of the group.

(g) Develops a sympathetic understanding and appreciation of one or more people who have different language and customs where conditions permit.

(h) Tries to find examples of what he has learned about culture in the social and aesthetic values of his community.

(i) Uses accurate generalizations in describing groups which differ from his own.

(j) Has sufficient awareness of his own values and tastes to select group leisure-time activities from which he derives keen enjoyment.*

(k) Has enough awareness of what is going on in the world to understand group discussions and to participate in them.*

Developmental Equivalents for 2.22

(Expectations for younger or less mature students)

Is learning how to resolve differences and to understand them.

Begins to learn how to stand up for his principles, even when teased about them.

Discusses differences of views or of purposes amicably.

Develops friendships with his own and the opposite sex.

Participates in discussions in groups without being rude or careless.

Is beginning to establish satisfactory heterosexual relations after going through a period of attachment to the same sex.

ORGANIZATION OF PROPOSED OUTCOMES

Seeks out people who can help him become more at ease in social groups and help him develop his interests.

Is developing the social skills necessary to contribute to parties.

Can introduce strangers with suitable form of address according to age, sex, etc.

Acknowledges and gives a salute on meeting acquaintances.

Lets elders and women (if a boy) enter a room first and stands until they are seated.

Shows courtesy in holding open a door or, at the table, holding a chair (a boy for a woman or a girl for an older woman).

Thanks a host or hostess on leaving a party or ending a visit.

Is beginning to value open-mindedness as an attitude in listening.

Is growing in willingness to desire and to understand the point of view of the other fellow.

Is beginning to find satisfaction in some of the arts as a medium of expression.

Explores the various arts, sampling many ideas and patterns of expression.

Begins to organize his social conversation around topics of group interest and to avoid embarrassing topics.

Shares his thinking with others in informal conversation and panel discussions.

Is able to state an individual opinion contrary to those of his friends in group discussion.

Begins to classify behavior as "good" or "bad" and "acceptable" and "unacceptable."

2.23 Utilizing Various Kinds of Competence Needed by Members of Small Organized Community Groups.

2.231 Is especially careful to apply the principle of full respect for personality toward small community subgroups when they represent cultural, racial, and religious interests different from his own.

Illustrative Behaviors

(a) Understands something of the different subgroups in his community—their similarities and differences and their contributions to community life.*

(b) Understands some of the contributions of different ethnic groups to the American way of life and that the plurality of the cultures composing the community add richly to community life.*

(c) Enjoys friendships with members of racial and religious groups different from his own.

BEHAVIORAL GOALS OF GENERAL EDUCATION

(d) Refrains from a self-righteous attitude toward those whose standards of right and wrong differ from his.

(e) Tries to recognize his own prejudices and attempts to overcome and eliminate them.

(f) Does not speak disparagingly of others because of differences of race, ethnic origin, religion, or social class.*

(g) Understands the civil liberties embodied in our bill of rights.

(h) Works to extend civil rights and liberties to all persons regardless of race, religion, ethnic, or socioeconomic origin.

(i) Recognizes that integration is in keeping with American ideals and works within the social context to achieve it.

(j) Deplores quota systems which discriminate against members of any group, such as college quotas, club quotas, job quotas, and works to get such systems abolished.

(k) Applies in his face-to-face contacts an understanding of the democratic rights, privileges, and responsibilities of citizens of the United States.

(l) Defends the right of each individual to follow his own religious beliefs.

2.232 Exercises as a student interested in civic and political affairs, or as a junior member of such groups in the community, the civil rights to which he is entitled, defends them for others, and assumes the responsibilities of a young citizen.

Illustrative Behaviors

(a) Recognizes his responsibility as a citizen or future citizen to stand for the maintenance of the constitutional rights of all citizens in his community.*

(b) Recognizes that no right is absolute and that all rights are limited when they interfere with other rights.*

(c) Recognizes the right of individuals to own, control, and use private property.*

(d) Recognizes that public interest, necessity, and welfare determine whether or not the rights of the public to own, control, and use property can be exercised, regulated, and restricted.

(e) Recognizes the importance of freedom of speech and of the press to the preservation of democracy, and defends these rights in his face-to-face relationships and in school and community decisions.*

ORGANIZATION OF PROPOSED OUTCOMES

(f) Recognizes free access to knowledge as the keystone of democracy and stands for the right of the people in his school and community to get the facts on controversial issues.

(g) Stands for and defends the right of each individual to worship God in his own way or refrain from religious affiliation or beliefs.*

(h) Respects and obeys constituted authority in school and community.*

2.233 Is actively interested in the problems faced by the school and community, and works in appropriate ways as a member of the student body and of community groups.

Illustrative Behaviors

(a) Studies, reads about, and discusses the main issues in bond elections and referendums and other community affairs.

(b) Understands his responsibilities, as well as his privileges, in the community and in the local units of government under which he lives.*

(c) Knows something about what makes communities "good" ones in which to live, and is actively interested to make and to keep his community a "good" community.*

(d) Understands some of the problems faced by modern cities, and the need for community planning.*

(e) Knows and appreciates the services performed for him by community agencies and institutions, and knows how to get more information about them if needed.*

(f) Helps a group arrive at conclusions about courses of action in discussion of problems of the community.*

(g) Identifies problems of the community that need attention and wherever possible proposes solutions.

(h) Urges parents and neighbors to vote in elections.

(i) Knows the techniques for political action which can be used legitimately by young people in attacking community problems.

(j) Knows the methods of taking political action at the community level.

(k) Writes an intelligible letter to the editor of a local paper when this seems to be a channel through which he can appropriately express a significant point of view.

153

BEHAVIORAL GOALS OF GENERAL EDUCATION

(l) Contributes freely from experience gained in school projects when participating in community projects.*

(m) Works with others to protect the natural beauty spots in the community from commercialization and deface-ment.

(n) Approves community efforts to provide facilities for worthy use of leisure time and supports them in appro-priate ways.

(o) Recognizes the value to the community of a community band, orchestra, little theater, choral group, and other kinds of cultural groups; participates in them according to his ability and contributes to their support with his interest, attendance, time, and money.

(p) Has some understanding of how communities finance their governments and services.*

(q) Understands his obligations and privileges in the school community.*

(r) Shows some recognition of the fact that a sound pro-gram of education involves social, emotional, and physical growth or change, as well as intellectual growth; and that it ought to be available to the elderly as well as the young in the community.*

(s) Is able to help others become informed about the need for better or additional educational facilities in his school.

(t) Has some appreciation of the fact that democratic edu-cation gives students an opportunity to seek the truth, to investigate all the evidence, to reach their own deci-sions; and is thus able to sense the differences between education and indoctrination and propaganda.*

(u) Knows why we have compulsory education and abides by its requirements.

2.234 Understands the role of religious organizations and of other organized groups with social service, or ethical interests and programs; and joins them or otherwise expresses his constructive interest in their efforts in his community.

Illustrative Behaviors

(a) Understands something of the major aims and objectives of various religious and ethical groups within the com-munity and respects their different customs and rituals.

(b) Takes a stand for social service projects through which any group seeks to apply democratic, spiritual, or ethical principles.

ORGANIZATION OF PROPOSED OUTCOMES

(c) Understands the welfare services available in the community and, if he can, gives some of his time or spending money to promote their programs.

(d) Works with others to discourage the support of cheap or degrading motion pictures, stage shows, or newsstand literature.

(e) Works for adequate financial support for public education, public library services, etc., as befits one of his age.

(f) Is gaining a concept of what a sound program of public education is trying to accomplish in the area of ethical and moral standards. On his own level of maturity, uses his influence, where he can, to interpret these purposes.

(g) Acts upon his beliefs—religious, ethical, moral, and social—while defending the right of others to different beliefs.

(h) Is interested in the part religion plays in human life and accepts the right of others to have a religion different from his own.

(i) Participates in religious and spiritual activities within the community.

(j) Recognizes the basic force of religions among people of the world; their differences and contributions to individual security and a wholesome society.

Developmental Equivalents for 2.23

(Expectations for younger or less mature students)

Gets practice in leading discussions.

Begins to develop group, not gang, loyalty (based on goals which are accepted by society).

Stays away from undesirable gangs or unwholesome places.

Shows developing skills and personality factors which make him an acceptable member of a democratic social order, especially in cooperativeness and open-mindedness.

Tries to test out the ideas he has of democracy in his everyday group living.

Votes, runs for homeroom offices, serves on committees for school plays and activities.

Helps to set up codes for behavior and for membership in organizations.

Is gaining experience in presiding over small groups with guidance by teachers and family.

Learns how candidates are chosen, laws passed, and issues settled.

Belongs to clubs outside school (YM-YWCA, Scouts, interest clubs, music and dance groups, etc.), and learns to apply school standards of behavior.

BEHAVIORAL GOALS OF GENERAL EDUCATION

Brings exhibits and collections to school and describes them.

Is able to give and follow directions, explanations, descriptions, and announcements with facility.

Is discovering what kind of contributions he can successfully make in group activities.

Carries on his share of the group's plan.

Recognizes the different functions and responsibilities of the various officers of a club or other organization.

Serves as chairman or member of a committee.

Can see differences and learn how to differ without giving offense or showing intolerance.

Is beginning to realize the importance of searching for and using data pertinent to the solution of a problem.

Understands the need for community laws and rules.

2.3 Developing Behaviors Involved in Maintaining Physical and Mental Health and Safety in Small (Face-to-Face) Group Situations.

Behavioral outcomes to be sought from general education because of the desirability of being able and willing to participate with others in maintaining and creating healthful and safe living conditions in one's home, school, and neighborhood.

2.31 Maintaining Health in the Home.

2.311 Does his share to contribute to physical health and safety in the home and family situation.

Illustrative Behaviors

(a) Avoids, as far as possible, close physical contact with members of the family when he is feeling ill; uses only his own toilet articles, etc.

(b) Keeps the home and its premises clean and sanitary and strives for healthful environment in the home.

(c) Understands need to live up to sanitary standards in preparing and serving meals and in preserving leftovers and other foods, and helps in doing so.

(d) Helps when needed in the care of sick members of the family; follows doctor's instructions.

(e) Demonstrates conscious concern to prevent accidents and fires in the home by putting things in their proper places; reporting appliances needing repair or repair-

ORGANIZATION OF PROPOSED OUTCOMES

ing them himself; avoiding careless use of electrical equipment; disposing of rubbish; caring for fire extinguishers, etc.

(f) Lives up to safety precautions in driving the family car.*

(g) Helps to keep poisonous and other injurious substances properly labeled and stored in safe places.

(h) Is aware of safety hazards in the home, and acts to minimize them.

2.312 Tries to maintain and promote family mental health.

Illustrative Behaviors

(a) Knows some of the basic facts about mental health and applies them to family relations and child rearing and to participation in family living.*

(b) Sees the family not only as an economic unit, but as a psychological unit in which creation of individual personalities is the chief function.

(c) Learns to accept some of the limitations of his parents and siblings without undue frustration or self-pity.

(d) Participates with the entire family in a balanced recreational program for all.

(e) Participates easily in activities with younger members of the family and adjusts to those of older members of the family and of their friends.

(f) Frequently and at appropriate times gives verbal expression to members of the family of affection sincerely felt for them.

(g) Is increasingly able to discuss important matters with parents and to disagree with them without becoming emotionally upset.

(h) Feels responsible for contributing his share toward maintaining the good name of the family.

(i) Is gaining a better understanding of the fact that sound family relationships are essential to emotional stability.

(j) Assumes his proper share of the family chores, including gardening, housekeeping, making minor repairs.

Developmental Equivalents for 2.31

(Expectations for younger or less mature students)

Realizes that his actions can affect the standing of his family in the community.

Participates in a family recreation program.

Begins to tolerate graciously and with a degree of pleasure the companionship of younger or older members of the family and their friends.

BEHAVIORAL GOALS OF GENERAL EDUCATION

Assists with planning, preparation, and serving of family meals.

Observes high standards of personal cleanliness; washes his hands frequently, especially before meals.

Maintains adequate concentration and diffusion of artificial light for reading.

Contributes by example to the regularity of meals at home, at school, or elsewhere.

Recognizes need for regular and sufficient sleep.

Recognizes the danger of handling uncovered wires, radio tubes, etc., when the current is on.

Recognizes the odor of escaping gas and realizes its danger.

Guards against misuse of electric fuses or overloading the electric circuit.

Sees that electric cords and connections are secure and protected.

Removes oily cloths, refuse, and other fire-hazards.

Refrains from monopolizing the phone, the bathroom, the radio, television, etc.

Respects the privacy of family members. (Never opens another's mail; knocks before entering a closed room, etc.)

Shows some signs of rivalry with siblings, but controls himself quite well in this respect.

Beginning to have good table manners.

Has to be reminded and sometimes urged to do his home chores.

Sees that poisons and medicines are labeled.

2.32 Maintaining Health as a Participant in Small Peer-Groups.

2.321 Recognizes need to maintain physical health in small peer-group situations, and contributes toward its attainment.

Illustrative Behaviors

(a) Avoids exposing self or others to colds or other diseases during the period when they are infectious; disposes promptly of used paper handkerchiefs and napkins.

(b) Behaves in a way that shows concern for the cleanliness, sanitation, and proper use of public buildings; takes the initiative in a group for cleanliness of environment; and gives consideration to health factors involved in group activities.*

   (c) Uses no habit-forming drugs and helps any group of which he is a member toward this behavior.

   (d) Knows something about the way communicable diseases are prevented and controlled, and therefore recognizes the importance of quarantine laws, insect and rodent control, inspection of food, milk, and water, etc., and supports community efforts exerted toward that end.

   (e) Avoids the type of rough-housing, tripping, and other types of potentially dangerous play which may lead to injury.

2.322 Begins to recognize need for, and to contribute to, mental health in small peer-group situations.

Illustrative Behaviors

   (a) Is growing increasingly aware of the degree to which cooperation rather than competition encourages creativity, growth in human welfare, and the spirit of democratic interaction and endeavors to have all participate.

   (b) Has friends as well as acquaintances in both sexes.

   (c) Accepts social responsibility of own sex on dates. (Boys assume responsibility for safety, respect for wishes of "date," financial obligations, etc. Girls are considerate of boys' financial position and assume responsibility for helping to plan and carry out activities on dates, etc.)

   (d) In situations in which his classmates exhibit anger, destructiveness, poor sportsmanship, or other unwholesome behavior, begins to think about what may lie behind the behavior and to understand the need of these classmates for friendship and acceptance.

   (e) Accepts graciously the success of others.

   (f) Will adjust personal interests for the sake of the group.

   (g) Knows and is friendly with most other members of one or more groups.

   (h) Exhibits the necessary forcefulness while serving as a group leader.

   (i) Tries to control and redirect his impulses when people or situations tempt him to react intemperately or violently.

   (j) Recognizes the group solidarity and true friendships that can be built by sharing sports and other activities; offers as good competition as he can and exhibits good sportsmanship.

BEHAVIORAL GOALS OF GENERAL EDUCATION

(k) Engages in activities and behavior which give him a sense of belonging to the peer group.*

(l) Meets his basic needs for belonging, for releasing tensions, for achievement, and for affection in socially constructive ways. Is sensitive to these needs in others and helps to build and maintain an environment in which they may be increasingly satisfied.*

(m) Begins to understand the damage done to personality when lines are drawn between a supposedly socially superior in-group and a supposedly socially inferior out-group.*

(n) Shows some understanding of the psychological needs which lie behind the behavior of his friends and acquaintances.*

(o) Treats those with handicaps and thwarted development with respect and understanding, and goes out of his way to help everyone in a group to participate in activities and to feel comfortable and at home.

(p) Is learning the importance of calmness in a crisis and of sufficient control of his fears and anxieties; does not unduly affect associates.*

(q) Accepts criticism intended to be helpful; gives criticism graciously.*

(r) Appreciates the value of the balance of work and play, of social entertaining skillfully, of vacations and leisure.

(s) Appreciates the great world of nature and the outdoors as resources for mental and spiritual, as well as physical, rejuvenation.

(t) Enters into school affairs (parties, dances, picnics) with concern both for his own good time and for the enjoyment of the other young people involved.

(u) Helps the group resolve conflict situations in order to avoid feelings of defeat and defiance on the part of some members.

(v) Lends his support to school policies which encourage wide participation in student activities.

(w) Refrains from identifying himself with a group or club which encourages divisiveness or snobbery.

(x) Recognizes that his natural resistance to adult domination is part of his growth toward maturity, and with increasing confidence in himself is learning to live with parents and other adults on more equal terms than formerly.*

ORGANIZATION OF PROPOSED OUTCOMES

(y)   Searches out and allies himself with older people (real and fictional) whom he can love and respect and who can help him strengthen his ideals and face life with courage and a sense of adventure.

(z)   Seeks to increase community interest in teenage problems of recreation and education.

Developmental Equivalents for 2.32

(Expectations for younger or less mature students)

Comes to see what causes handicaps and underdevelopment and has a feeling of tolerance.

Curbs any envy that may arise from success of another in the group.

Is beginning to sense that individuals can influence group behavior.

Refrains from smoking or drinking even when invited or when other members of his group take part.

Observes safe behavior as a passenger in his family or friends' cars.

Always uses safety skills in the water (never changes seats in a boat or dives in unknown spots, etc.).

Turns away and covers mouth and nose when coughing and sneezing.

Learns to play many indoor games and to play them when others desire.

Participates in games and sports in small groups at school, home, and church.

Learns what it means to be a good sportsman.

Seeks or accepts a date with poise and minimum embarrassment.

Learns to control his temper and to behave intelligently when he does not get his own way.

Is practicing honesty in schoolroom as well as in extracurricular activities.

Accepts criticism of his peers and adults without being vindictive.

Develops the personal qualities which contribute to personal attractiveness and charm: interest in other people, generosity, friendliness, enthusiasm, good humor, etc.

Understands the reasons for variance of growth among his friends and refrains from unkind teasing.

Avoids all labeling and name-calling which results in hurt feelings or which classifies people without regard for their qualities as individuals.

Gains sufficient enjoyment from his classroom and extra-class activities to eliminate his need for engaging in cut-throat competition for grades and awards.

Helps new pupils in his classroom or club meet other pupils; shows them "the ropes" and helps them feel wanted.

2.33 Contributing to Health and Safety in Small Group Situations in School and Community.

2.331 Recognizes importance of community safety programs and facilities, and cooperates in their maintenance and development.

Illustrative Behaviors

(a) Recognizes the importance of providing for hospital and medical expenses by saving money, by carrying accident and sickness insurance, or by joining a voluntary health insurance plan.

(b) Understands the needs for and evaluates community health services, such as clinics, hospitals, home-nursing services, and care for the handicapped and aged.

(c) Recognizes society's responsibility for providing hospital care and rehabilitation to the emotionally and mentally ill.

(d) Understands the relationship of community centers and recreation clubs to the mental health of the people in the community.

(e) Understands and abides by safety rules regarding the use of the swimming pool and other recreational facilities, and observes them willingly.

(f) Obeys traffic laws and fire and air-raid drill regulations established for the protection of groups.

(g) Is familiar with the program and practices of, and gives his support to, such agencies for accident prevention and disaster control as the police and fire departments, Civil Defense, the American Red Cross, and the National Safety Council.

(h) Conforms to the safety and health rules for the use of public parks, beaches, playgrounds, and other community recreational facilities.

2.332 Recognizes the need for community control of health conditions.

Illustrative Behaviors

(a) Understands the functions of the public health agencies and appreciates their activities.

(b) Knows and observes the health and safety rules of the school. *

(c) Evaluates the school plant in terms of a healthful environment and works to eliminate hazards to health and safety.

162

ORGANIZATION OF PROPOSED OUTCOMES

(d) Understands and appreciates the measures taken by the school to protect his health.

(e) Appreciates the services of, and cooperates with, the custodial staff in keeping the school building clean, safe, in good repair, and properly ventilated.

(f) Understands the need for the collection of vital statistics in the community and uses them to study the health problems of the community.

(g) Recognizes the need for sewage disposal, public water safety, inspection of eating establishments, and other public health and safety measures.

(h) Understands the effect of poor housing upon the health and safety of people who live in substandard homes and the danger to the whole community.

(i) Recognizes the need for parks and recreation facilities and works for an adequate recreation program for the community.

Developmental Equivalents for 2.33

(Expectations for younger or less mature students)

Begins to be careful in use of public buildings, parks, playgrounds, and other facilities.

Avoids membership in a high school fraternity or other exclusive school, church, or community group whose membership is based solely upon social popularity.

Adjusts to the presence of several peer groups within the school and the neighborhood.

Uses public recreational facilities properly.

Learns about social institutions for mental illness and their value.

Learns about the Pure Food and Drug Act and its regulations, and recognizes their value.

Learns the value of such organizations as the Boys' Club, YMCA and YWCA, and Scouts for young people.

Recognizes the health hazards of modern city life and works to reduce them.

Recognizes the relationship of sanitation to public health.

Refrains from contaminating the water supply and observes regulations.

Accepts the need for inoculations to prevent the spread of disease.

Cooperates willingly in school and community efforts to set up civil defense activities.

Feels his responsibility for obeying and enforcing local safety and health regulations.

BEHAVIORAL GOALS OF GENERAL EDUCATION

2.4   Developing Behaviors Indicative of Growth Toward Economic Competence and Independence in Small Group Situations.

Behavioral outcomes to be sought from general education because of the need to participate intelligently and effectively in the discussion of, and decisions upon, economic matters in one's family, school activities, neighborhood organizations, and groups of fellow-workers.

2.41 **Improving Economic Competence and Independence in Family and Small Group Situations.**

2.411 Participates and cooperates in family financial matters.

Illustrative Behaviors

(a)   Adjusts his demands for financial outlays from parents' earnings to other family needs and its income.

(b)   Is able to cooperate with the family, if permitted, in planning and budgeting for recreational activities, family vacations, and special expenditures not classified as necessities.

(c)   Recognizes the importance of savings in the family income.

(d)   Wherever his experience permits, tries to help parents on problems for which they assume the responsibility for the family, home modernization, income tax, consumer buying, etc.

(e)   Accepts with good spirit limited space and facilities which depend upon present family budget.

(f)   Assumes his proper share in family decision-making on matters of budget.

(g)   Through part-time or summer employment, begins to accept a reasonable share of responsibility for his financial needs.

(h)   Helps the family maintain a sound credit rating by not expecting to charge items without family knowledge.

(i)   Is learning how to shop wisely to get the most from the family dollar.*

(j)   Cooperates with the family in the maintenance and repair of the home.

(k)   Recognizes that different types of occupations and professions influence the kind of home life one can have or maintain for one's family and applies this to the family situation.

ORGANIZATION OF PROPOSED OUTCOMES

(l)   Begins to understand the advantages and disadvantages of home-ownership.*

(m) Recognizes that the job of managing a home in today's changing world calls for understandings, attitudes, skills, and teamwork for which individuals need adequate preparation.*

2.412 Recognizes need for being an economically intelligent member of the family and of small groups to which he belongs.

Illustrative Behaviors

(a) Recognizes need to pay bills promptly, and if that is not possible, to explain the difficulty and work out a mutually satisfactory plan of payment.

(b) Understands the importance to the family of life, fire, storm, and liability insurance, the advantages and disadvantages of it, and something of the various types of policies which may be secured.

(c) Knows the types of lending agencies in a community and the advantages and disadvantages of each.

(d) Knows the advantages and disadvantages of installment buying.*

(e) Knows that family savings help to make possible expenditures for large items, such as homes, automobiles, and travel.

(f) Sees need for family to keep records of business transactions so that difficulties which may arise can be handled in a businesslike and courteous manner.

(g) Is able to read graphs and charts dealing with economic matters.

(h) Understands the business activities and the financial needs of the groups of which he is a member and lends his support to worthy projects; favors only expenditures which can be met out of the group's resources.

(i) Is sufficiently familiar with the basic principles of practical finance to take a tenable and socially responsible stand on some of the debatable economic issues in school, club, or community groups.

(j) Contributes to charitable groups (even out of a small allowance). Spends some money on others.

(k) Assumes financial responsibility for his share of joint expenses on dates, at school parties, for school publications, and class dues; and meets these obligations promptly.*

BEHAVIORAL GOALS OF GENERAL EDUCATION

Developmental Equivalents for 2.41

(Expectations for younger or less mature students)

Is developing some understanding of why some families do not have as well-equipped homes as others.

Helps to plan expenditures for clothes, whether or not included in an allowance, with a balanced view of needs and a limited total.

Saves money from an allowance over a period of time for a special purpose, or at least occasionally works for a while to earn money for a special purpose.

Follows instructions in handling costly and fragile equipment.

Calculates the cost of borrowing money at various interest rates.

Explains in general terms the purposes of different kinds of insurance.

Is aware of the liabilities of the car-owner and driver for personal injury and property damage and of the safeguards.

Identifies the various taxes on family income and property.

Shops on a given occasion for food and other household supplies within the limit of the cash provided for the purpose.

Cooperates with the family in reducing food waste.

Cooperates in conserving heat and light.

With the assistance of his parents collects and uses helpful information in making purchasing decisions.

Is beginning to appreciate the fact that the income of the family has limits which must be taken into account.

Develops a respect for quality and price in his own purchases.

Chooses goods and services as well as he can, profiting by advice of family and friends.

Accepts willingly his share of work in the home and is beginning to see the relationship of his contribution to the economic welfare of the family as a whole.

Listens to family discussions on household economics and actively participates when they concern him.

Begins to understand the purposes which social security and pension plans serve.

Does his share in helping to keep family expenses within a budget.

2.42 Becoming a Good Member of Work-Groups.

> 2.421 Is concerned that groups exercise care in economic matters.
>
> **Illustrative Behaviors**
>
> (a) Appreciates the work of service clubs and similar groups in encouraging the business and economic growth of the community and in protecting both business and the consumer.
>
> (b) Has had work experience in some sort of small group operation—a group of store clerks, a gang of laborers, a

ship's crew, an office staff, community service organizations, school service group, etc.

(c) Shares with other employees his knowledge of any conditions and facts which may lead to intelligent decisions by them.

(d) Appreciates property protection provided by the agencies of local government.

(e) Recognizes the economic as well as social reasons for child labor laws and other laws related to labor-management relationships.*

(f) Sees that discrimination in the labor market, because of race, sex, religion, or ethnic origin is an economically unsound practice, as well as being socially and morally wrong.*

(g) Shows a sense of social responsibility in conserving school supplies and protecting school and other public property.*

2.422 Begins to recognize and assume the rights and responsibilities of members of work-groups.

Illustrative Behaviors

(a) Uses properly and keeps in good order the tools and equipment shared by a class or other group to which he belongs.*

(b) Is prompt, cooperative, and generally compliant in carrying out reasonable instructions on a job.*

(c) Is reliable in doing a job even when unsupervised. Does not merely make a pretense of working.*

(d) Feels responsible for giving a good day's work for a day's pay.*

(e) Has an attitude of responsibility toward his work which others in the group can count on.*

(f) Has learned how to make a report of his work-results with clarity and simplicity.*

(g) Is learning how to give criticism directly to people pleasantly and in terms they understand and accept.

(h) Demonstrates his belief that members of labor unions or business groups should strive to be ethical and fair in the stand they take on labor-management issues.

(i) Knows why labor has the right to organize and bargain collectively and favors it.*

BEHAVIORAL GOALS OF GENERAL EDUCATION

(j) Condemns violence as a means of settling economic problems of labor disputes.*

(k) Knows why he should take an active part in the activities of the workers, if employed in an "organized" industry.

(l) Shows his understanding of the effect of collective support and pressure for desired legislative action on labor and other economic matters.*

(m) Participates in school activities in such a way as to develop and demonstrate ability to work well with others.*

(n) Accepts his share in a cooperative project even though it may not have as much glamour as someone else's.

(o) Identifies himself with groups that can help him prepare for economic independence.

(p) Respects those with whom he works and shows some understanding and consideration for them.*

(q) Reads about and discusses some of the economic forces that may affect his vocational life (new discoveries and inventions in business and industry—changing standards and opportunities in professions—and problems of production and distribution of goods and services.)*

(r) Can and does assume leadership in a work-group when his ability and experience justify it.*

(s) Scrutinizes the policies of the various business groups operating in the community and refuses to give support to those whose special interests conflict with community interests.

(t) Understands the relationships between the economic security of the community and its industrial expansion.

Developmental Equivalents for 2.42

(Expectations for younger or less mature students)

Participates in panel discussions on junior high school level dealing with goods and commodities.

Displays promptness and courtesy in complying with reasonable requests.

Begins to appreciate relationship between employee and employer.

Feels responsibility for work he undertakes, but sometimes lacks judgment in carrying it through.

Comes to understand pressure-group actions.

Reads about and discusses some of the new discoveries and inventions in the world of business and industry that are continually changing man's vocational opportunities.

ORGANIZATION OF PROPOSED OUTCOMES

Gets some informal experience in small work-groups under adult direction.

Makes tentative efforts at leadership in a small work-group, some of which are successful.

Assumes some financial responsibility in a small circle of membership, such as Boy or Girl Scouts.

Meets his financial obligations (dues, assessments, etc.) to group promptly.

Learns to inhibit prejudices toward nationality, race, color, or religion of fellow workers.

Defends the rights of all groups to educational and work opportunities.

Is punctual in his working hours.

Willingly works on committees and participates in drives to make money for school projects.

2.43 Manifesting Interest and Participation in the Economic Affairs of the Community.

2.431 Holds some opinions on economic affairs of the community and its organizations and institutions based on his study of them.

Illustrative Behaviors

(a) Knows what jobs are available in the community, trends in employment, and the requirements and opportunities for various jobs.

(b) Willingly works on committees and participates in drives for worthy community projects if asked to do so.

(c) Recognizes the importance of free public education for all and of opportunity for continued vocational education for all workers of the community.

(d) Is informed about community needs for public funds and lends his influence with his friends and associates for the support of justified expenditures for public education and welfare agencies and other services which will promote the welfare of the community.*

(e) Knows how the government and services of his community are financed and something of the economic structure of his community.*

(f) Recognizes that the community tax rate should be set at a figure which provides for the efficient operation and continuance of such government services as the community desires.

BEHAVIORAL GOALS OF GENERAL EDUCATION

2.432 Takes an interest and participates in groups concerned about the community's use, management, and conservation of its natural resources.

Illustrative Behaviors

(a) Is interested in working with others to protect woodlands from fire, and plant and animal life from careless or ruthless destruction.*

(b) Takes some initiative in school and community groups to correct false notions which lead to the destruction of desirable plant and animal life.

(c) If he engages with others in such sports as hunting and fishing, he does so in accordance with conservation laws and without wanton destruction of wildlife, and stands for enforcement of such laws.

(d) Takes some initiative in school and community groups to eliminate destructive plant and insect life.

(e) Opposes the commercialization of beauty spots.

(f) Is acquainted with and eager to help solve the community's major problems relating to water power, parks, etc.

(g) Is interested in the community's educational facilities (schools, libraries, etc.) as a major factor in the wise use of human resources.

Developmental Equivalents for 2.43

(Expectations for younger or less mature students)

Reads and understands some statistics dealing with business.

Can calculate roughly the level of tax on the basis of actual or hypothetical figures.

Has some understanding of the sanctity of a contract.

Beginning to learn about statements of assets and liabilities and can determine whether these statements balance.

Studies the nature, extent, and value of public education.

Engages with others in school and community projects that involve planting cover crops to stop erosion, reforesting, controlling pests, etc.

Observes and studies the relationship between labor and management in his community.

Learns something about the way public opinion is formed on economic and other public matters in his community.

Begins to sense the economic dependence of his family upon the other persons in the community, of businesses upon other businesses, and of his community upon other communities near and far.

Sets an example with his associates by engaging in good camping and picnicking practices: care of fire, garbage, etc.

3. **GROWING IN ABILITY TO MAINTAIN THE RELATIONSHIPS IMPOSED BY MEMBERSHIP IN LARGE ORGANIZATIONS.**

Many of the varied activities of modern man take place in large religious, cultural, social, political, and economic organizations. The successful functioning of these large groups arises not so much from the intricacies of their organizational structure as from the intelligent, effective, cooperative, and devoted service of their constituent members. Education for responsible citizenship in a free society through general education in high school therefore needs to be broadly interpreted to include preparation for intelligent evaluation of the purposes and plans of these large groups; opportunity for practice in effective participation in them through the mastery of the legitimate techniques and skills by which their decisions are reached; and the cultivation of a spirit of willingness to give wholehearted service to those groups to which one chooses to belong.

3.1 Developing Behaviors Indicative of Intellectual Growth and Development.

Behavioral outcomes to be sought from general education because responsible and effective participation in the deliberations of large political, cultural, economic, and industrial groups and intelligent action in such groups require the full use of one's intellectual powers.

3.11 Becoming Intellectually Able to Follow Developments on the World and National Levels and to Formulate Opinions About Proposed Solutions to Some of the Principal Problems and Issues.

3.111 Is developing an interest in, and understanding of, world events, conditions, and organizations.

Illustrative Behaviors

(a) Recognizes that survival demands that the peoples of the world learn to live together without war; is aware of the more likely preventives of war, and supports by word and deed as occasion permits efforts to make these operative.*

(b) Recognizes conditions and problems in his own and other countries which threaten world peace; supports measures to improve such conditions and approves of measures for helping the peoples of underdeveloped areas to improve their standards of living.*

(c) Understands why no national state, such as the United States, can alone fortify itself adequately against the threat of a foreign power; realizes that the United States must ally itself militarily and economically with the free or would-be-free nations that have the courage to resist imperialism.

(d) Supports efforts of international agencies, such as the United Nations, to reduce poverty, ignorance, and disease in underdeveloped countries by acceptable means.

(e) Recognizes that some type of world integration is desirable and studies the various possibilities of achieving more effective integration.

(f) Knows and contrasts some of the basic concepts and practices of democratic and totalitarian states concerning: family life, morality and religion, schools and formal education, government and political parties, economic organization and regulation, civil liberties and rights, public opinion, and class differences.*

(g) Examines critically proposed measures for international control of atomic weapons and disarmament.*

(h) Accepts obligation to serve in the armed forces and to support the nation's defense program in order to check aggressors and prevent war unless this is contrary to conscience.

(i) Gradually begins to recognize fundamental differences in people and learns to understand and live with them amicably: (a) develops respect for them; (b) recognizes his own prejudices and tries to control them; (c) seeks to develop some common interests with those who are different.*

(j) Identifies himself sufficiently with people of different nations and cultures to have a desire to understand their viewpoints and policies on international questions, and is interested in movements which help to interpret to Americans the goals, cultures, and problems of other nations.*

ORGANIZATION OF PROPOSED OUTCOMES

(k) Recognizes that social changes usually take place in a slow, evolutionary manner; that resistance to change or too rapid change may produce revolutions and social upheavals, and may produce more suffering than benefits to mankind.*

(l) Expresses disapproval of values inconsistent with the welfare of individuals generally and with those inconsistent with democratic principles.

(m) Expresses approval of changes in national policies which promote international cooperation when such changes are in harmony with democratic principles and will further world peace.*

(n) Understands the difficulties of achieving the principles and goals of democratic nations in foreign relations when dealing with totalitarian governments which believe ends justify means, and recognizes the need for a trained, experienced diplomatic corps.*

(o) Understands how the culture and way of life of a people are affected by the topography, climate, and natural resources of their physical environment.*

(p) Recognizes the responsibility which the United States because of its wealth and power must assume for leadership in international affairs and for the promotion of world peace.*

(q) Sees the problems which his country faces in international affairs as of great concern to him and seeks to have a part in their solution.

(r) Recognizes that the primary aim of a nation's foreign policy is the protection of its welfare and sovereignty.*

(s) Realizes that Russia extends its domination by persuasion only in the initial phase of its penetration; that thereafter it quickly seeks to take over all the agencies of control, and when it succeeds in doing so, ruthlessly utilizes these agencies to dominate the people concerned.

(t) Understands the geography of the world sufficiently to place accurately areas of worldwide importance (areas in the major news).*

(u) Knows the major racial groups in the world and their origins, and can place them in their geographical relationships.

173

BEHAVIORAL GOALS OF GENERAL EDUCATION

3.112 Endeavors to become well informed on the backgrounds of the larger problems of our nation and the world and to make an intelligent analysis of the issues involved.

Illustrative Behaviors

(a) Enters into study and discussion of controversial issues (political, economic, and social; local, national, and international) with a willingness to look at all sides of the controversy and weigh consequences in terms of conscious values.

(b) Recognizes that change is inevitable; that cultures and institutions which fail to adjust to changing conditions decline and are replaced by more adaptable cultures and institutions.

(c) Is learning to apply the advances of science to community organization and planning (transportation, communication, employment) and such other community problems as can be similarly studied.

(d) On the basis of his knowledge of world's geography and its people, examines the evidence concerned with the so-called "superiority" or so-called "inferiority" of any group.

(e) Understands and can explain adequately enough of the world's different social customs to document the view that "there is no one way of adapting to one's environment."

(f) Knows that most of the world's peoples have for centuries fatalistically suffered personal indignity, poverty, hunger, and disease, but that they are now rapidly acquiring the belief that they are not necessarily bound to their present lot.*

(g) Reflects upon the chief characteristics of American ideology and uses this frame of reference in analyzing the national and international issues on which he must take a stand.*

(h) Believes that everyone has the responsibility of keeping informed about public problems and of the actions taken on them by those in public office.*

(i) Follows legislative programs in city, state, and national legislatures and in the United Nations in order to be able to express considered opinions to his representatives and to others when he feels it important to do so.

(j) Reads magazines and books which discuss national and world issues and keeps informed on current problems and issues of national, religious, political, cultural, economic, and industrial groups.

(k) Is familiar with most of the world and national figures currently and in the past.

(l) Identifies certain social values as desirable for all peoples; e.g., loyalty, political freedom, economic opportunity, education, etc.*

(m) Knows the significance of the general facts of economic, political, and social history of his country.*

(n) Understands and can explain to others how the welfare of the nation is related to his own personal welfare and to theirs.

(o) Expects social change in his own country and has faith that it can be intelligently directed toward democratic goals through democratic means.*

(p) Is trying to develop informed opinions on the major issues of social and governmental policy at the national level; e.g., farm income, immigration, civil rights, natural resources, labor-capital relations, financing of public education.*

(q) Learns how people in other lands live, the nature of their problems, what they do for us, and what we do for them, and how important it is that we work with them.*

(r) Studies his own values and tries to harmonize them with others, with the broad stream of human thought, and with the realities of the contemporary social scene.

(s) Makes discerning judgments on the reliability and completeness of information available in newspapers, magazines, books, radio, television, forums, lectures, and discussion groups.*

(t) Listens frequently to programs on radio and TV presented by individuals in leadership positions and designed to acquaint the public with various points of view on public issues.

(u) Is interested in, and recognizes the value of, acquiring some historical perspective on the broad social and economic problems in the solution of which he is participating.*

Developmental Equivalents for 3.11

(Expectations for younger or less mature students)

Senses the importance of problems of war and peace, and desires to learn more concerning what can be done about them.

Knows the facts of national history and understands the implications of some of them.

175

BEHAVIORAL GOALS OF GENERAL EDUCATION

Has only a limited conception of what social change is, but is gradually increasing it.

Is beginning to get the idea that his own personal welfare is related to that of the nation.

Is beginning to see that he has a stake in the United Nations and the work of ICA, UNICEF, and UNESCO.

Is beginning to realize that his own happiness and welfare, and that of his family, may depend on what is happening in other countries of the world.

Begins to see the interdependence of the world scientifically and culturally for knowledge, ideas, and values.

Understands how science and technology have increased the speed and ease of transportation and communication.

Can recognize some situations in which the standard of living in the United States is dependent upon trade with foreign countries.

Understands something about the organization and function of the United Nations and its agencies.

Sometimes recognizes that conditions which breed misery, discontent, and conflict in any part of the world are a threat to his own peace and security.

Senses the imperative need for national defense and supports it, but also supports world peace.

Knows that most people know little about people in lands other than their own, and seeks ways to achieve greater understanding.

Learns the major differences between communism, fascism, socialism, Hitlerism, dictatorship in Spain, and the United States government. Learns the rights of people under such forms of government.

Eliminates from his vocabulary all derogatory "type-names," such as "niggers," "kikes," "dagos," "wops," "wags," "flips," "frogs," "fish eaters," etc.

Understands that civilizations that have destroyed human rights have always fallen.

Develops an understanding that racial, religious, ethnic, and any other type of bigotry, prejudice, or discrimination are enemies of peace and, hence, of mankind.

Begins to study and think about current national and international problems in terms of the issues at stake; e.g., desegregation, public power, sale of the public domain, teacher shortage.

Participates with his classmates in analyzing some of the national issues which especially affect teenagers in order to isolate the issues.

Has some information about important national news but does not always keep informed.

176

ORGANIZATION OF PROPOSED OUTCOMES

Reads about national defense and understands need for it today.

Can identify the major nations on a world map.

Can identify the major races on a world map.

Understands some of the democratic traditions and objectives in American life and the personal obligation of citizens to the state and nation.

Is beginning to realize that modern life has its origin in the past and that clues to the meanings of modern life may be sought in the past as well as in the present.

Is beginning to grasp the story of the United States and its significance in the evolving history of mankind.

3.12 Identifying Himself with Large Groups and Organizations Interested in Cultural, Social, Economic, and Political Affairs, and Becoming an Effective Member of Them.

3.121 Is an intelligent and active member, at least on a "junior" level, of large groups and organizations.

Illustrative Behaviors

(a) Selects with discrimination a few organizations with which he wishes to be active and encourages others to select those in keeping with their major concerns.*

(b) Recognizes the need to participate responsibly in the programs and policies of large groups, either in support or opposition, because he realizes how such groups affect the actions of individuals and small groups and the welfare of the nation.

(c) Recognizes the value of working with a political party or organization to formulate appropriate policies for dealing with other nations.

(d) Supports the idea of international cooperation through such principles as are set forth in the United Nations.

(e) Recognizes the weakness of the arguments of the communistic or wholly nationalistic philosophy as a solution to economic conditions abroad.

(f) Joins with others in promoting understanding of public issues through organizations concerned with public enlightenment.

(g) Expresses his opinions in writing on matters of great moment to the appropriate members of local, state, or federal government and to government agencies, citing facts and arguments and using clear, forceful, and courteous language.

BEHAVIORAL GOALS OF GENERAL EDUCATION

(h) Takes into account the effect of a practice of one group on the welfare of other groups; establishes priorities of values in deciding on the soundness of a proposal of a large group.*

(i) Works in, with, and through groups to crystallize and agree upon goals and to convey his desires to those in positions of responsibility.

(j) Respects the right of other groups to work toward goals in which he is not interested and with which he may not agree.

(k) Takes an active part in some major school and community functions and organizations and can carry some responsibility for some aspect of their activities.

(l) Is interested in community conditions and plans for the future, and has some knowledge of its history and traditions which he uses as background for his thinking about these conditions and plans.

(m) Exemplifies good citizenship by abiding by the regulations of the school and its organizations and works to make them realistic and functional.*

(n) Is able to conduct a business meeting of a large group or, as a member, knows when a meeting is being properly conducted, using such conventions as rules of order, if, as, and when these facilitate group thinking and acting.

(o) Recognizes that he has a personal interest and responsibility in community problems involving essential services providing for the welfare of the entire community.

(p) Uses persuasion and objective argument in his group endeavors as opposed to arbitrary and violently emotionalized actions.

(q) Exhibits freedom from prejudicial emotional behavior in working for action.

(r) Lets his precinct or ward leader, or county committeeman, know his views on prospective nominees if suitable means can be found.

(s) Works when among the minority to get a fair consideration of its position in the hope of changing the majority's decision.

(t) Learns to work with people; to be mannerly, gracious, and emotionally balanced; to accept decisions and policies when agreed upon; and to analyze causes of failure and success.

ORGANIZATION OF PROPOSED OUTCOMES

3.122 Exercises rights and duties in political organizations when permitted, and gains increasing understanding of democratic policies and procedures.

Illustrative Behaviors

(a) Participates in school political activities and elections.*

(b) Understands the structure and operation of local, state, federal, and international government, and is learning to fix responsibility with reasonable accuracy, to express grievances, and to make effective use of personal influence.*

(c) Takes the initiative when necessary and possible to secure social legislation in the interest of equality of opportunity for all persons.

(d) Expresses his opinions to members of government for actions, statements, and decisions of which he strongly approves or disapproves.

(e) Votes when eligible in all elections in which he believes there is a reasonably significant choice between issues or candidates.*

(f) Is growing in the realization that means and ends are indivisible, that democratic means must be used for democratic ends, and that every effort must be made to correct injustices by legal action or persuasion before there is resort to force or violence.

(g) Accepts the basic idea of government by majority decision and does not as a minority ignore or violate a law or decision made by the majority unless contrary to conscience; urges the testing of such matters in the courts.*

(h) Understands that as people demand more services of their government, government becomes more complex and costly.

(i) Evaluates his community government in terms of its contribution to the quality of living for families who reside there: protection, cultural stimulation, educational and recreational opportunities.*

(j) Evaluates the leadership and services of local, state, and national governments in terms of their preserving opportunities for private initiative and at the same time providing for governmental activities or cooperative efforts when necessary to serve public needs.*

179

BEHAVIORAL GOALS OF GENERAL EDUCATION

(k) Takes pride in being a member of the community and thinks of himself as being a citizen with some responsibility.*

(l) Has some objective knowledge and thinks critically about political forces and issues operating in his local community and how these affect his life.*

(m) Understands the political party setup in this country and the ways in which an individual can influence public affairs as a regular party member or as an independent, and is interested in being an active participant in public affairs.*

(n) Seeks to become informed on the policies and competencies of competing candidates for municipal, state, and national office.*

(o) Accepts as a responsibility, participation in elections even though his age precludes actual voting at this time.

(p) Is becoming able to decide which, if any, political party he favors in local, state, or national elections, based upon the stand taken on the issues he favors or opposes and upon the quality of the candidates offered.

(q) Visits legislatures, courts, and other governmental institutions when possible, to gain first-hand experience with them.

(r) Is willing to submit his own ideas to examination by fellow members of his class, or of his work or political group.*

(s) Subjects the recommendations of groups to intelligent analysis before he accepts them as his own.*

(t) Cooperates with school, neighborhood, or community groups in identifying common problems to be solved, in gathering pertinent facts, in making plans for solutions of problems, and in carrying out action jointly recommended.*

(u) Understands the purposes of government and how the national and state governments use their productive, regulatory, and promotional powers to establish justice, preserve the peace, provide for the common defense, promote the general welfare, and safeguard individual freedom.

(v) Understands the reasons for separation of powers among the three branches of the national government and how the system of checks and balances operates.

(w) Recognizes the necessity for bureaucracy in local, state, and national governments with many and complicated functions, but also the problems and dangers of bureaucracy in government.*

ORGANIZATION OF PROPOSED OUTCOMES

3.123 Has some understanding of the way public opinion is formed; uses defensible methods in helping to form it; and guards against being victimized by the indefensible methods of others.

Illustrative Behaviors

(a) Seeks to separate fact from opinion in the verbal controversies in progress and does quite well in analyzing propaganda.*

(b) Understands what is meant by public opinion, its influence, and the part of each individual in its formation.*

(c) Understands that an informed and constructive public opinion depends in large degree upon free access to all information and upon the free expression of conflicting opinions through open public discussions and mass media communication: press, radio, TV, and motion pictures.*

(d) Recognizes the forces influencing public opinion and the effect of public opinion in shaping and controlling group action.

(e) Assumes responsibility for seeing that the publicly expressed opinion of the groups to which he belongs accurately reflects the opinion of at least the majority of the members.*

(f) Comes to know the ways in which the community becomes informed, devices used to influence people, the means sometimes used to mislead people, and how to prevent abuses.*

(g) Recognizes and differentiates between legitimate and unwarranted pressure tactics to influence local, state, national, and world policy and action.*

Developmental Equivalents for 3.12

(Expectations for younger or less mature students)

Is beginning to understand how people working together creatively can find new approaches and solutions to community, national, and world problems—solutions that cannot be found any other way.

Is growing in understanding of the reasons for having institutions, such as schools, libraries, courts, health departments, etc.

Is becoming aware of the work and structure of government; visits the legislature of his state or the council of his town or city.

Is beginning to take an interest in problems and issues of religious, political, cultural, economic, and industrial groups.

Is beginning to realize that his personal life is affected by the policies and practices of large groups.

BEHAVIORAL GOALS OF GENERAL EDUCATION

Takes part in major school functions for his age-group; may be somewhat shy about participating in those dominated by upperclassmen.

Active on occasion in a community youth activity; e.g., Scout drives for wastepaper, Junior Red Cross solicitations, etc.

Is sympathetic to school regulations and tries to abide by them.

Works rather well in committees, but may need help in organizing and following up details.

Senses the importance of making his point of view known prior to the time a decision is reached and then being a good sport in abiding by the decision even though it does not please him.

Knows who the major political figures (president, governor, mayor) are, but is only beginning to concern himself much with political issues.

Is beginning to question the validity for him of group decisions in which he has no share.

Is beginning to sense that individuals make up groups and that, therefore, well-educated individuals are important to the welfare of large groups.

Senses that a good citizen should participate in large groups and should serve as a leader where his abilities permit.

Learns to talk before class and student organizations.

Is learning to conduct a class meeting, using Robert's Rules of Order where they help the group get its business transacted.

Discovers that successful large group meetings require careful planning by individuals who are willing to give of their time and ability.

Takes some interest in following political campaigns and election results.

Does some community service without expecting remuneration.

Uses resources with increasing skill in finding facts to support opinions and arguments.

Professes democratic attitudes toward others and acts accordingly, but when crises arise sometimes "goes with the crowd."

Is concerned about problems of delinquency.

3.13 Evidencing Intelligent Appreciation and Support of Democratic Goals and Principles and of American Cultural, Social, and Political Traditions.

3.131 Appreciates and respects democratic goals and principles and political traditions in American life.

Illustrative Behaviors

(a) Accepts and acts upon the principle that decisions made by free people who have access to the facts and the factors involved are better in the long run than decisions made by one man or a group of men.*

(b) Leads others to accept the principle that the welfare of all is a measure of the success of democracy.

ORGANIZATION OF PROPOSED OUTCOMES

(c) Believes in the use of reasonable negotiation rather than the use of force to settle differences.

(d) Recognizes that there is a place for the expert both in decision-making and in carrying out the decisions of the people.

(e) Believes that legal action should be taken by the government to prevent slander and deliberate misrepresentation of individuals or groups.

(f) Is motivated primarily by those moral and spiritual values that are a part of all religious faiths, as well as by those that are more sectarian in origin.

(g) Supports in every possible way all movements that he believes are sincerely aiming at the preservation and extension of constitutional rights for all.

(h) Obeys the law and the rules adopted by the group and is aware of the price paid by conscientious objectors to certain laws.

(i) Has some understanding of the place of faith in human relationships.

(j) Learns about religious beliefs, differences in religious faiths, in churches, and their program; attends and participates in church or nonchurch activities for his age level where these matters are considered.

(k) Recognizes the need for improved programs of public elementary, secondary, and higher education and for its increased support, because equality of educational opportunity underlies all other equality of opportunity and because of its role in helping to educate an electorate competent and enlightened enough to make wise decisions on increasingly complicated issues.*

(l) Has a sense of worth and destiny in belonging to the United States of America and to the United Nations with its worldwide program of human betterment.*

(m) Upholds basic constitutional principles, such as the separation of church and state and equality before the law of all citizens.*

(n) Operates on the principle that every human being has dignity and worth and is deserving of respect in his own right regardless of race, nationality, religion, or the socioeconomic groups to which he belongs, and uses this principle in judging state and national policies.*

(o) Recognizes the discrepancies between democratic ideals and practices, but recognizes the progress toward these ideals and works to strengthen and extend the application of democratic principles to all citizens and to all aspects of life.*

BEHAVIORAL GOALS OF GENERAL EDUCATION

(p) Exhibits democratic attitudes in interaction with other socioeconomic, religious, and racial groups and will stand up for groups that are attacked on the basis of such differences.

(q) Complies with the spirit as well as the letter of the laws as he understands them.*

(r) Supports the principle of government by law, and respects and obeys law enforcement officials.*

(s) Understands the meaning of perjury.*

(t) Rejects membership in any organizations or groups that operate outside the law, or that set themselves up as self-appointed agencies for law enforcement and works to destroy such organizations.*

(u) Works with others to educate people to obey laws.*

(v) Believes that the rights of citizenship and its privileges cannot be denied or abridged because of race, origin, or religion, and works to see that such rights are adequately protected for all.

(w) Evaluates and supports political issues or national problems in terms of what seems to be the greatest good for the greatest number.

(x) Performs services without pay which may be needed for preserving the common welfare (in flood, fires, or other disasters) or which promote the common welfare (serving on committees, engaging in welfare work, participating in political organizations, performing community services, etc.).

(y) Considers himself and all other people equal members of the human race and rejects racism as a national or international policy.

Developmental Equivalents for 3.13

(Expectations for younger or less mature students)

Is beginning to learn skills in handling controversy through persuasion and legitimate compromise, rather than through force.

Knows that there are several major political parties which stand on somewhat different platforms.

Questions any statement which purports to attribute special vices or virtues to a specific national, racial, or religious group. Asks for the evidence on which such statements are made.

Realizes that some communities are better places in which to live than others and is trying to determine why.

184

ORGANIZATION OF PROPOSED OUTCOMES

Just beginning to show an attitude of responsibility for welfare of local community.

Recognizes a difference between fact and opinion but may sometimes be satisfied with a substitution of one for the other.

Is beginning to realize the importance of free speech and expression in large group participation.

Is in general agreement with policies of student government and tries to abide by them.

Asks some questions about community problems, especially those affecting his activities.

Is beginning to understand the role of men and women who serve the people as "public servants"—the policeman, the fireman, the teacher, the lawmaker, the judge, and elective officers.

Understands how laws are established and modified, and is interested in whether a law is passed, defeated, amended, or repealed.

Is interested in learning about people who are candidates for political office and about those who are officers of large groups.

Supports rights against injustice.

Understands that democracy is government from the "bottom up" and that "we" are the government.

Begins to be able to detect propaganda and to identify propaganda techniques.

Understands the difference between being a "citizen" and a "subject."

Treats those he meets in a bus, in a shop or restaurant, or in a home as equals, whatever their social or economic position.

Appreciates the role of public education in a democracy and the importance of its continued improvement and support.

Shows some interest in discovering the kinds of values which are common to all religious groups.

Begins to be critical of any proposal that involves the idea that any group of people have special privileges because of birth, place of origin, residence, wealth, or race.

Knows the rights guaranteed by the Constitution and has some understanding of the reasons they are guaranteed.

Recognizes to some extent why free political parties are essential to the growth of democratic institutions in this country.

Begins to recognize that in a democracy individual liberty is legitimately limited when it interferes with the common welfare and accepts willingly this limitation upon his freedom.

Abides by laws pertinent to his age-group, but may often do so just to avoid trouble for himself.

185

BEHAVIORAL GOALS OF GENERAL EDUCATION

3.2   Developing Behaviors Indicative of Growth Toward Cultural
Orientation and Integration.

Behavioral outcomes to be sought from general education because the responsibilities of membership in large group organizations are often best discharged when proposed policies, programs, and activities are reviewed against their cultural backgrounds or in the light of ethical and aesthetic standards and
values.

3.21 Viewing Current Events and Conditions in This Country and in the World in the Light of Their Historic and Cultural Pasts.

3.211 Is able to relate some principal world problems and
situations of our day to events and conditions of the past.

Illustrative Behaviors

(a) Sees important current events (such as the development of great labor organizations, America's increased
participation in world affairs, the decline of colonialism,
the awakening of underdeveloped countries, the struggle
of the American Negro for equality, and other contemporary world problems) in historical perspective. *

(b) Has a general knowledge of the historical development
of the most important great civilizations.

(c) Appreciates the struggles, sacrifices, and achievements of
the courageous and freedom-loving people who made our
nation possible and built it into the great nation it is today.

(d) Has general knowledge about the population, natural
resources, economy, and political structure of the following segments of the world: Middle East, Africa,
India, China, Southern Asia, Soviet Union, Western
Europe, South America, Australia.

(e) Recognizes the impossibility of continuing a policy of
isolation in today's interdependent world. *

(f) Knows the general facts about the United Nations and
its more important specialized agencies, and understands the purposes and ideals. *

(g) Understands American ideals, customs, traditions, and
symbols and takes pride in his national heritage, based
upon a knowledge of its achievements. *

(h) Is interested in being somewhat acquainted with the development of cultures of various people of the world
and the relationship of these cultures to his own social
institutions, religion, arts, government, ways of making
a living, use of the land, family life, etc. *

ORGANIZATION OF PROPOSED OUTCOMES

(i)   Is interested in the contributions of the various old world cultures to American life. *

(j)   Spends some of his time and effort to gain a broader and more sympathetic understanding of the peoples of other lands. *

(k)   Is aware of national, racial, religious, and "other groups" stereotypes and their vicious effects in creating misunderstanding, suspicion, distrust, and discrimination, and attempts to divest himself and others of these distortions. *

(l)   Believes that the "way of life" of some other nations may be as good for them as that of our own nation is for us.

(m) Gains increased insight into social, political, economic, and personal problems by seeing the relationship between problems presented in fiction and drama depicting the past and those of real life today.

(n)   Recognizes that many national customs which originated as rational and satisfying ways of meeting needs became institutionalized and continued to be valued even though conditions have changed. These often appear irrational and peculiar to an outsider who does not understand their origin.

Developmental Equivalents for 3.21

(Expectations for younger or less mature students)

Begins to see that present culture is a development of past civilizations.

Knows that all parts of the world are not like his community but has only vague notions about differences and unique features of various sectors.

Thinks nations must cooperate to avoid war, but has little idea of any specific machinery that might accomplish this.

Occasionally shows some genuine interest and concern for problems of international scope.

Knows that there are different religious practices in some other parts of the world.

Has but little notion of the relation of his personal welfare to international cooperation.

Begins to recognize the democratic heritage and to value it.

Learns about the differences in countries with and without modern technology.

Begins to understand that the culture—the pattern of living accepted by members of a group—is learned, not inherited.

Begins to recognize that there are more similarities than differences in cultures.

Appreciates the contributions which people of different races, nationalities, and religions have made and continue to make to the American way of life.

BEHAVIORAL GOALS OF GENERAL EDUCATION

Is learning about community living in other parts of the world.
Tries to distinguish between the areas appropriate for governmental
and voluntary community support, and to discover why this should be.
Often rebels at participation in rites and ceremonies, but comes to accept them as socially necessary and perhaps later even as personally
desirable.

3.22 Developing Cultural Background Through Reading and Participating in Various Cultural Organizations and Activities.

3.221 Reads and uses other means of communication to expand his knowledge and appreciation of his own and
other cultures.

Illustrative Behaviors

(a) Lives vicariously the life of the various culture groups
that make up America and of other cultures different
from our own through reading and other means of
communication.

(b) Reads widely in a variety of fields of literature to become acquainted with the various aspects of his culture.

(c) Builds cultural backgrounds by listening, observing,
and reacting to mass communication media (TV, radio,
press).*

(d) Reads the biographies and other available information
concerning persons who have lived and worked in the
public interest and thus enlarges his concept of community in both time and space.

3.222 Is interested in, joins, or supports a few organizations
of various types as a way of getting a variety of cultural
experiences and appreciations.

Illustrative Behaviors

(a) Learns about the development, nature of differences,
ways of working, and importance of political parties in
other countries.

(b) Cooperates in community drives to establish a library
or in developing art or music studios, or exhibit rooms
in school which are freely available to students.

(c) Joins groups in protest of the treatment of minorities
and initiates and supports measures designed to reduce
tensions.

(d) Tries to become informed about the purposes and effectiveness of world organizations, such as UNESCO, etc.*

188

ORGANIZATION OF PROPOSED OUTCOMES

(e) Supports community welfare agencies by money or other contributions, and is willing to work in their drives and campaigns.

(f) Advocates a balance between volunteer agency work and government humanitarian and social service work.

(g) Learns about services of Red Cross, recreational agencies, United Crusade, Community Chest, and other local agencies (their worth, what they cost, and how to support them).*

(h) Investigates and knows about some of the national and international groups and movements whose objectives are humanitarian (Friends' Service Organization, CARE, etc.).

(i) Is learning to appreciate the contributions which the artists of other nations as well as America have made to his enjoyment of music and art and to the cultural entertainment of all people.*

(j) Shows an understanding of the desirability of musical and artistic activities in the community and is interested in evidences of general community support.*

(k) Wants the community to respect beauty and order in community planning.*

(l) Upholds honesty, duty, impartiality, and similar virtues in public office, and supports the activities of civic groups designed to promote such ideals.*

(m) Accepts religion as one of the great centers of human interest and tries to understand what effect it has on the lives of his contemporaries.*

(n) Works with others to plan for church-related or social service activities and helps in carrying out such plans.

(o) Is developing considerable interest in the meaning and value of a life of service to humanity.*

(p) Is actively interested in seeing his community act in harmony with a high standard of ethical behavior.

(q) Begins to understand what is involved for the citizen in applying individual ethical standards to public issues (what is involved in public morality).*

(r) Is familiar with the working philosophy of some of the great spiritual leaders of the world as background for deciding how and where to use his efforts and to throw the weight of his opinion.*

(s) Practices the tenets of moral and spiritual living by engaging in constructive and wholesome activities with groups at a continually expanding level.

(t) Participates in activities designed to improve the moral and spiritual position of his peer groups.

BEHAVIORAL GOALS OF GENERAL EDUCATION

Developmental Equivalents for 3.22

(Expectations for younger or less mature students)

Depends upon his vicarious experiences for understanding or insight into large group behaviors, such as strikes, panics, conventions.

Participates in church, camping, conference programs.

Accepts religion rather completely on the basis of practice by adults.

Reads some of the literary works of other countries' great authors, poets, and dramatists.

Beginning to read in newspapers and magazines items about national and international events and problems.

Is becoming more cosmopolitan and catholic in his attitudes.

Is beginning to understand that there are many constructive forces in a community that have a good influence; e.g., those that result from the work of community councils, youth councils, recreation centers, counseling service.

Patronizes good local youth programs.

Allies himself with one or more groups through which he can make his influence felt to improve the quality of human relations.

Seeks to contribute to the beauty of his home and his neighborhood.

Shows some sensitivity to high ethical standards by the stand he takes on school and community issues and problems.

3.23 Seeing Vocational Activities in Their Cultural Settings.

3.231 Recognizes his chosen life-work not only as a means of support but as his way of making a contribution to his country and the world.

Illustrative Behaviors

(a) He considers a vocation from the standpoint of service to his fellow men as well as from its financial possibilities.*

(b) Discusses lucidly the place and value of his chosen career in the greater society.

(c) Works consistently well because he believes that the quality of his work will have an effect upon the status of his chosen profession or vocation.*

(d) Is interested in learning more about the standing of his prospective vocation in the community and the nation, and watches its action where morals and ethics are involved.*

(e) Knows the primary vocational groups of importance in his own community and studies the attitudes and actions of those most nearly related to his own vocational choices.

(f) Follows the work of national organizations that contribute to the welfare of his chosen field and tries to keep in touch with their actions as they relate to moral and ethical matters.

(g) Recognizes the effect of the national culture on the status of vocational groups, ways of doing things, and standards.

Developmental Equivalents for 3.23

(Expectations for younger or less mature students)

Realizes that public or group benefits; e.g., sick leave, workman's compensation, sickness and accident insurance, unemployment insurance, should not be misused.

Recognizes that a vocation makes a contribution to the well-being of individuals, groups, and society.

Is beginning to be aware of the ways in which his vocational activities can contribute to larger groups, in addition to his immediate home, school, and community.

Reacts toward the needs of society by thinking of specializing in a particular field of knowledge, skill, or service.

3.3   Developing Behaviors Indicative of Understanding Problems of Mental and Physical Health.

Behavioral outcomes to be sought from general education because of the need for cooperating with other members of large organizations in reaching decisions on matters that affect the mental, emotional, and physical health, and the safety of whole communities, states, the nation, and the world.

3.31 Recognizing Health as a World Problem, and Supporting Worldwide Scientific and Humanitarian Efforts and Organizations.

3.311 Supports various worldwide organizations working to improve world health conditions and standards.

Illustrative Behaviors

(a) Appreciates the strides so far made in eliminating hunger, disease, and ignorance in the world. Supports this work through agencies and activities of our federal government, through agencies sponsored by the United Nations, by churches, and by other agencies, such as CARE, the Junior Red Cross, and the Friends' Service Committee.

(b) Recognizes the importance of the work of the Commission on Narcotic Drugs of the United Nations in controlling traffic in narcotics.

BEHAVIORAL GOALS OF GENERAL EDUCATION

(c) Appreciates the work of UNICEF in controlling communicable childhood diseases; in combating deficiency diseases by providing milk, fats, fish-liver oil, and meat; and in educating families in underdeveloped areas in the value of good nutrition for children.

(d) Evaluates the work of WHO and other United Nations agencies in protecting and improving the health of people, particularly in underdeveloped areas.

(e) Is sensitive to the humanitarian implications of the problems of surplus food commodities and approves a policy designed to permit their use in ways that will benefit those who are ill-fed and ill-clothed.*

(f) Has some measure of understanding of the destruction of life wrought by modern warfare and uses his influence as a citizen to reduce the hazards of war.*

(g) Considers the implications for human welfare of such inventions and discoveries as atomic energy, jet propulsion, hydrogen bombs, biological warfare, and brain washing.

(h) Acquires sufficient background in the areas of human biology, anthropology, and psychology to develop an increased understanding of the physical and emotional needs of human beings the world over.

(i) Through reading, viewing, and listening to accounts of the health conditions in the nation and world, begins to feel some responsibility for national and worldwide health and sanitation and some identification with those who suffer from unwholesome living conditions.

(j) Begins to understand the geographic, economic, cultural, and political factors which result in widespread malnutrition in many parts of the world.

(k) Evaluates plans for alleviating shortages in medical care and supports those plans with which he is in sympathy.

3.312 Understands the roles of research and political action in solving public health problems.

Illustrative Behaviors

(a) Understands and shows an affirmative attitude toward the goals and work of scientific groups engaged in medical research to prevent and cure our most ravaging diseases: heart diseases, arteriosclerosis, infantile paralysis, cancer, cerebral palsy.

(b) Is willing to participate in local campaigns to raise money for research on health problems.

ORGANIZATION OF PROPOSED OUTCOMES

(c) Learns something about the ways in which research has contributed to the improvement of food, the care of the sick, and the conquering of many diseases, and understands that political action is necessary to ensure these benefits being used properly.

(d) Understands that much work needs to be done by public and private health agencies so that people will use the knowledge now possessed to improve health and health conditions in general, and joins with others to use political means where necessary to influence action.

(e) Examines various proposals for making adequate medical care available to all, through both public and private agencies, and supports those which he believes most effective for the purpose.

(f) Understands the part that United States can play in helping to improve the health of people in the underdeveloped areas of the world.

(g) Understands the values, and advocates the use locally and nationally of scientific discoveries in protecting and improving health, such as Salk vaccine, fluoridation of water, etc.

Developmental Equivalents for 3.31

(Expectations for younger or less mature students)

Is becoming aware of some of the needs of children in our society and is recognizing a few problems which some senior citizens are experiencing.

Has some knowledge of the regulations of the Pure Food and Drug Act, and recognizes their importance.

Seeks information regarding measures which are in operation, and others that may be needed for the improvement of community health.

Understands the need for immigration procedures, port quarantine, etc.

Includes in his newspaper and magazine reading at least some articles dealing with general problems of physical and mental health.

Is aware of his responsibility to support laws and regulations that require honest labeling and information to safeguard the public.

Reads about new health discoveries and talks to groups about them.

Understands the need for research in the killer diseases and helps others become interested.

Is becoming aware of the need for improved protective measures; e.g., food inspection, sanitary food handling, safety controls.

Recognizes scientific progress is being made and envisions future progress.

BEHAVIORAL GOALS OF GENERAL EDUCATION

3.32 **Appreciating and Supporting Work and Services of Federal, State, and Local Health and Safety Departments, and of Volunteer Organizations.**

3.321 Appreciates and supports work of federal, state, and volunteer agencies in the field of public health.

Illustrative Behaviors

(a) Learns the importance of health service and the part governments can take in it.

(b) Seeks protective health and safety legislation through group action.

(c) Supports government activities in enforcing health standards.

(d) Disapproves of discriminatory practices in health services.

(e) Is aware of the need for greater health protection for all citizens and is challenged by the problems generated by increasing costs of medical care.

(f) Knows the ways in which meat inspection and the Pure Food and Drug Act protect his health.

(g) Recognizes the shortage in some areas of doctors, dentists, nurses, and hospitals as a national problem.

(h) Recognizes the work done by national health organizations in carrying on research on the cause and cure of specific diseases and in aiding those stricken with the disease.

(i) Works for protective laws for youth: health, accident, and preventing immoral conditions.

(j) Understands the reasons underlying sound legislation requiring certain types of insurance to protect those receiving injuries (workman's compensation insurance, automobile liability insurance, etc.); supports such legislation and complies with it.

(k) Understands that the United States Public Health Service protects him against communicable diseases by interstate quarantines and by preventive measures such as testing drinking water and controlling disease-carrying insects and rodents.

(l) Appreciates the importance of the medical and hospital care provided by the United States government for veterans and men in the armed services.

(m) Appreciates the importance of the Social Security program to the health of the nation.

194

ORGANIZATION OF PROPOSED OUTCOMES

(n) Works with groups to secure passage of protective laws, together with their enforcement, against accidents, improper health conditions, and business misrepresentations.

(o) Gives consideration to the grant-in-aid program to the states in caring for the needy blind, needy children, crippled children, and needy old persons, and in providing maternal and child health services, child welfare services, and public health services.

3.322 Is constructively interested in and supports organized community health and safety programs and activities.

Illustrative Behaviors

(a) Feels personally responsible for preventing the spread of diseases and acts accordingly.

(b) Cooperates with others in the prevention and relief of poverty in his community.

(c) Where necessary, will cooperate in community efforts to remove the causes of difficulty with alcohol, narcotics, and other drugs.

(d) Cooperates with others in the community to promote public health education and to secure proper public health conditions by law, by enforcement of such laws, and by proper financial support of governmental and voluntary agencies.

(e) Recognizes and is critical of propaganda for the sale of products that might affect community health adversely.

(f) Promotes measures for fire prevention. Reports to proper authorities promptly any hazardous conditions he observes in his school or in the community.*

(g) Recognizes organized sports and games as a means of promoting physical and mental public health, and favors adequate local provisions for them.

(h) Supports community drives for recreational facilities for children.*

(i) Recognizes an unduly emotionalized crowd and does not join in its actions (a dispute over a decision in baseball, basketball, etc.).

(j) Uses high standards and humane consideration in his evaluation of group sports. (He disapproves of boxing for children and any sport that involves cruelty to animals, health or safety hazards for participants or spectators).

BEHAVIORAL GOALS OF GENERAL EDUCATION

(k) Encourages more provision for physical activity for children and youth than is at present generally available in many communities.

(l) Appreciates the value of physical fitness for national defense and understands the potential relationship between sports and good character development for youth and assumes leadership in community agencies which foster it.

3.323 Supports organizations and programs designed to provide highway safety and to prevent accidents and disasters in the community and in industry.

Illustrative Behaviors

(a) Is a member of a civil defense organization, or recognizes the importance of it enough to cooperate in civil defense activities.

(b) Recognizes the need for greater uniformity in traffic laws and in the enforcement of traffic regulations as one means of reducing traffic accidents, and cooperates with groups and organizations working for better laws and enforcement for traffic safety.*

(c) Appreciates the need for regulations to protect the public.

(d) Aids groups in securing proper police protection, industrial laws for accident prevention, properly marked highways, and safe road and building construction.

(e) Recognizes the need for state automobile insurance laws which require that all cars be insured to cover personal injury and property damage.

3.324 Recognizes the importance of mental health and the needs of the physically handicapped, and takes an active interest in such matters.

Illustrative Behaviors

(a) Recognizes the growing problem of mental health and gives all possible support to movements which encourage improved facilities for mental patients and more widespread public education regarding the problems of mental health.

(b) Informs himself concerning our national problem of mental illness and of the factors in our lives which often result in mental breakdown.

ORGANIZATION OF PROPOSED OUTCOMES

    (c)   Recognizes the need for better state mental hospitals and better state care for others suffering from long-term illnesses.

    (d)   Deals with, and thinks of, the mentally ill with the same understanding and sympathy that he shows toward the physically ill. *

    (e)   Gains conception of the public's responsibility for providing hospital facilities and appropriate medical care for the mentally ill.

    (f)   Knows about and supports public education for the physically handicapped.

Developmental Equivalents for 3.32

(Expectations for younger or less mature students)

Supports school health programs.

Understands the health work carried on by state governments.

Supports community efforts to remove the causes of difficulty with alcohol, narcotics, and other drugs. Will initiate efforts for community control where necessary.

Assists in and supports drives for funds, such as the "March of Dimes," Christmas sale of tuberculosis seals, Easter seals for crippled children, "Give to Fight Cancer," etc.

Cooperates in government inspection and regulations.

Is interested in regulations for the protection of the health of people in his community; complies with them and is willing to work with others for their improvement.

Is interested in learning something of what "good" housing means from the standpoint of the community, the state, and the nation.

Reads and listens with interest to accounts of juvenile delinquency; is able to discuss his personal views with others.

Accepts gracefully any personal inconvenience if it is necessary for the safety or health of the community.

Believes that safe driving laws should be enforced and cooperates with safety patrols.

Organizes car pools for parties to ensure there being only legal age drivers at the wheel.

Understands, supports, and complies with the municipal, state, and national traffic regulations which aim to reduce accidents.

Understands and complies with other legal regulations designed to guard against accident, such as building codes, licensing of firearms, etc.

Gains satisfaction from a sense of belonging and contributing to welfare groups in his school and community.

Refuses to contribute to a mass emotionalized action.

Refuses to support sports that exploit individuals or sacrifice animals.

Supports recreational activities of the community.

Has an interest in sports as a participant and spectator and is informed on the outstanding achievement in various sports.

Supports both varsity and intramural athletic programs.

3.4 Developing Behaviors Indicative of Growth Toward Economic Competence and Independence.

Behavioral outcomes to be sought from general education because of the responsibility of participating intelligently as a member of large political, economic, and industrial organizations in decisions as to how economic resources can best be managed in our society so as to permit expedient use of them but ensure their conservation.

3.41 **Recognizing the Worldwide Application of Economic Principles and the Economic Interdependence of the Peoples of the World.**

3.411 Recognizes interrelation of human welfare and economic life, and supports programs and organizations designed to recognize and act on these facts.

Illustrative Behaviors

(a) Shows awareness of the economic interdependence of people of his community, nation, and world. *

(b) Supports the right of each nation in the world to develop as well-balanced an economy as possible and to reduce economic fears, poverty, and unemployment. *

(c) Recognizes that differences in geographic environment and/or methods of production account for differences in levels of living in different times and places; e.g., in the United States today vs. the United States circa 1850, in the United States today vs. Egypt today. *

(d) Is aware that the needs of the world population are far in excess of the goods and services which are being produced at the present time and knows that even in this country millions of people are living below the minimum health and comfort level. *

(e) Evaluates the work of the commissions and agencies of the United Nations concerned with improving economic conditions in member and nonmember nations.

ORGANIZATION OF PROPOSED OUTCOMES

(f) Understands the need of undeveloped areas for foreign capital and critically examines the advantages and disadvantages in investment of private capital in those areas.

(g) Examines critically the various foreign aid proposals as means of making the benefits of our scientific advances and industrial progress available for the improvement and industrial growth of undeveloped areas.

(h) Recognizes that in a world of varying degrees of wealth, a rich nation like the United States may be required to make loans or gifts to the weaker or poorer nations.*

(i) Knows that the world population will probably increase sharply by 1980 and understands how the pressure of population on limited productive resources leads to competition among nations for land and trade areas and, hence, to international rivalries and tensions.

(j) Understands something about the relationship between national and international prosperity and the function of international and national agencies in promoting a more prosperous world economy.

(k) Understands the work of the International Bank and the International Monetary Fund of the United Nations in stabilizing the currencies of the nations of the world, in making and guaranteeing loans and investments, and in promoting the flow of capital internationally for productive purposes.

3.412 Knows something about the varying economic resources of different areas of the world, the different levels of productive ability, and the resulting standards of living; and sees the necessity for developing economic conditions and relationships which take these facts into account.

Illustrative Behaviors

(a) Understands the dependence of the United States on other nations and geographical areas for certain minerals and basic raw materials needed for national welfare or survival, and knows where the principal ones come from.*

(b) Understands the advantages of regional specialization in the world; that this makes the people in various national states economically interdependent and that a breakdown in one country tends to spread to others.*

(c) Understands that the development of the underdeveloped areas of the world makes possible the promotion
of world trade and goodwill by raising the standard of
living in such areas.

(d) Is informed of the economic needs of people in other
parts of the world and the relationship of these needs to
politics, government, and war.*

(e) Recognizes America's problem of maintaining our
standards of living while helping the world develop
economic relationships which permit high standards in
other countries.

(f) Recognizes the chief barriers to world trade and has some
knowledge of the nature and work of the agencies which
have been set up to promote international economic
cooperation. Is familiar with the outlines of our foreign
trade policy and is aware of the major foreign trade
problems which confront us.*

(g) Understands the importance of essential crops to our
industrial life and the need to import those not produced in the United States, or not produced in sufficient
quantities or cheaply enough to meet our industrial
needs; e.g., certain fibers, rubber, and industrial oils.*

(h) Understands the importance of food in international
trade.

(i) Evaluates the effect of trade restrictions on international
relations and world prosperity.

(j) Makes some thoughtful decisions which tend to relate
politics to the general welfare of all people.

(k) Understands the way tariffs may be used by one country
to protect its industries or to destroy industries in another country.

(l) Analyzes the economic implications of his contemplated
vote in national and local elections.

3.413 Recognizes the responsibilities of the United States for
leadership in settling world economic problems and
favors federal government programs designed to meet
these responsibilities.

Illustrative Behaviors

(a) Supports the government program of sending American
experts with American "know-how" into less developed
areas of the world, and of bringing experts from other
countries to this country to learn.*

(b) Understands the power of the United States over the
economic well-being of people in other countries; knows

that we generate about two-thirds of the world's total savings; that we are the largest single seller to, and buyer from, many countries that depend much more than we do on foreign trade; and believes that our actions can and should contribute to the stability and prosperity of the world economy.

(c) Knows why sufficient technical assistance and economic aid must be provided to enable the people of Africa, the Middle East, and Southeast Asia to secure for themselves adequate food, clothing, shelter, health, and hope for the future under conditions of personal dignity and freedom.

(d) Compares the role of government in regulating and controlling economic activity under the American capitalistic system with the role of government under other economic systems.

(e) Understands some of the possible effects of government control of international trade upon our own economy and the economy of the countries with which we trade.

3.414 Sees world trade as a means of promoting the economic welfare of the United States and of other countries, as a means of preventing war, as a way of promoting cultural interchange; and favors policies which promote world trade.

Illustrative Behaviors

(a) Recognizes that our military power and security depend in part upon access to the world's markets for strategic materials.

(b) Studies war and what causes it (what happens to people, to jobs, to resources, to consumer goods, to money during and after war).

(c) Sees world trade as necessary to maintaining economic well-being and to increasing the exchange of cultural ideas. *

(d) Recognizes the importance of world trade to the United States; the extent to which our industries depend upon foreign sources for materials; the importance of foreign markets to American business, industry, and agriculture; and the amount of employment which depends upon foreign trade. *

BEHAVIORAL GOALS OF GENERAL EDUCATION

(e) Understands that a consistent policy in foreign trade is necessary both for national prosperity and for building constructive friendship among free nations.*

(f) Recognizes that specialization of production in nations has resulted in multilateral trade involving many nations, necessitating international trade agreements and stabilized currencies.

(g) Can discuss some of the effects of barriers to free trade and the advantages and disadvantages of free trade in specific relation to protected industries.

(h) Recognizes that national self-sufficiency and military security may call for special protection of some domestic industries.

(i) Recognizes that both the exporting and the importing nation may benefit from the increased production made possible by international trade.

(j) Knows the political forces which back protective legislation but appreciates the problems they produce between countries.

Developmental Equivalents for 3.41

(Expectations for younger or less mature students)

Is growing in his understanding of the concept of interdependence in the economic world.

Is becoming aware of the heavy debt and poverty of some nations as a handicap to their progress.

Understands how American skill and "know-how" could aid less fully developed economies in other countries.

Is beginning to see the importance of world trade.

Begins to recognize that American prosperity is related to world prosperity.

Is beginning to understand how food is related to national security and international peace.

Recognizes that nations and areas produce particular goods and services with varying degrees of productive efficiency.

Knows the general outline of U.S. trade with other countries, but does not understand its full meaning.

Knows goods have to be paid for, becomes familiar in general with the idea of foreign exchange.

Begins to recognize the necessity for the United States buying from, as well as selling to, other countries.

Knows what a tariff is and senses something of how it works.

ORGANIZATION OF PROPOSED OUTCOMES

3.42 Supporting Measures of Federal, State, and Local Government, and Voluntary Organizations Designed to Conserve Human and Natural Resources.

3.421 Believes in the conservation of human and natural resources, practices it, and supports programs and organizations concerned with this national problem.

Illustrative Behaviors

(a) Believes in the use of natural resources for the good of the public and uses this as a criterion in reaching decisions on such matters.*

(b) Appreciates the achievements of science and technology in discovering new sources for the materials we are already using, in finding new and more efficient ways of extracting resources from known deposits, in finding uses for materials known but not usable, and in discovering and creating new resources.*

(c) Recognizes that all synthetics are produced from some natural resource and that their use does not lessen the need for conservation.*

(d) Defends the adequate provision of such activities by the federal government as the protection of national forests, game preserves, and the conservation of vital natural resources.

(e) Knows some of the methods used to conserve land and increase yield.

(f) Learns to work with groups to acquaint them with the need for concern over natural resources and their wise use.

(g) Recognizes that the stronger we become industrially and militarily, the greater drain there is on our mineral and other resources.*

(h) Recognizes the problem of potential water shortage, avoids misuse of water resources, and supports measures providing for regional planning for water use and for eliminating pollution of water.

(i) Appreciates the work of the Soil Conservation Service and other federal agencies, and of local and state agencies in helping to guard against depletion of resources

BEHAVIORAL GOALS OF GENERAL EDUCATION

and to restore to sustained productivity worn-out or damaged resources (land reclamation, flood control, reforestation, etc.); and supports such activities.*

(j) Acquires at least a minimum knowledge of economic geography, climatology, and animal biology as these relate to resources of food supply and their protection from ravage.*

(k) Understands something of the issues involved in public vs. private development of power, transportation, communication, etc., and takes a defensible stand in terms of the social welfare.*

(l) Recognizes the chief activities and products of his own region in relation to its resources and physical features, and appreciates the interdependence of different regions.*

Developmental Equivalents for 3.42

(Expectations for younger or less mature students)

Understands meaning of a "balanced economy" at home.

Is beginning to realize the economic influences involved in national, state, and local elections.

Begins to recognize that government aid to, and regulation of, business is necessary.

Becomes informed in a general way about government involvement in special projects (TVA, Soil Conservation, etc.).

Raises such questions as "why" concerning some employment restrictions.

Learns about laws concerned with child labor, unemployment, needless strikes, and workman's compensation; and knows their value.

Builds this understanding of the place and work and nature of employer and labor negotiations, labor unions, protection of working conditions, strikes, and other tools used by labor to protect themselves, as well as the work of government in protecting workers.

Understands the main features of the more important pieces of existing labor legislation; has some appreciation of its significance for labor unions, employers, and the public; and is aware of the ways in which the principal agencies of government which administer these laws function.

Compares arguments for and against governmental regulation of labor union practices and, in particular, strikes.

ORGANIZATION OF PROPOSED OUTCOMES

3.43 **Understanding the Need for Federal and State Governments' Stimulative and Regulatory Activities in Economic Matters and Affairs as Means of Making Our Free Enterprise System Work.**

3.431 Supports the principle of individual economic freedom which the free enterprise system is designed to provide and favors governmental activity designed to ensure the operation of this principle.

Illustrative Behaviors

(a) Studies various proposals for giving relief to hard-pressed economic and social groups, whether they be farmers, laborers, investors, white-collar workers, or victims of disaster; and supports any which he believes most effective for the purpose.*

(b) Believes that the individual citizen is responsible for supporting with his own private funds, as well as by taxation, such cultural and welfare institutions as the community chest, museums, symphony orchestras, and hospitals.

(c) Begins to understand how government may be used to aid farmers and industries and how some controls may hamper our free enterprise system.

(d) Demonstrates some understanding of the function of the federal government in maintaining economic stability by balanced credit, taxes, public works, employment, defense spending, and such other factors as are necessary.*

(e) Is aware of the actual patterns of the distribution of the ownership of natural resources and capital (partnerships, corporations, government and individual ownership) in this country and of the principal factors which tend to make these patterns what they are.

(f) Knows the kinds of restrictions government places on free enterprise and free competition (e.g., limitations on private property, on freedom of contract, on freedom of enterprise, on profit), and favors these as they tend to protect the economic freedom of individuals.*

(g) Knows something of the agencies and services of the national government concerned with regulating interstate commerce and communication, protecting the consumer, protecting our money and credit system and the buying and selling of securities, regulating business and preventing monopolies, regulating conditions between labor and management, regulating water power and public utilities, and controlling the use of atomic power; and views these as ways of providing the largest practicable zone of economic freedom to the largest number of individuals.*

(h) Understands how the government aids and promotes business by tariff regulations, by bounties and subsidies, by gathering and publishing information about business conditions here and abroad, by furnishing weather reports, by issuing patents, by standardizing weights and measures, and by carrying on research that is significant to industry; and favors such activities.*

(i) Understands how the national and state governments have aided labor through labor legislation, establishing a minimum wage, regulating hours of work, prohibiting child labor, enacting workman's compensation and unemployment insurance, and providing machinery for settling labor-management disputes; and supports such activities as means of promoting our economic welfare.*

(j) Appreciates the need for government regulation of monopolies, of antitrust laws, of laws protecting the public on investments and drugs, bank deposits, insurance, etc.*

(k) Understands that there is a cost to the consumer of "parity" and "fair trade" prices and takes this into account as he studies such practices.

3.432 Recognizes that there are situations and occasions when it is necessary and wise for federal, state, or local government to enter a productive activity, although it supports the principles underlying the free enterprise system.

Illustrative Behaviors

(a) Understands that the purpose of most of the productive activities of the government is to provide services for the public without profit in areas where business firms cannot operate profitably or where people believe they should not be allowed to operate.

(b) Appreciates the value of price controls during wartime, but understands also that the use of government by business to set prices is inconsistent with the principles of free enterprise.

ORGANIZATION OF PROPOSED OUTCOMES

(c) Evaluates measures affecting ownership use, and management of public lands and other natural resources in terms of how they will affect the general welfare of the nation.

(d) Understands the need for continued research by both government and private enterprise in the development and use of atomic energy for industrial and other constructive purposes.

(e) Accepts it as an obligation of the government to encourage prosperity among elements in our population, but recognizes the right of all men to differ on how government aid and coordination should be provided.*

(f) Recognizes that, in addition to setting up and enforcing the basic legal framework of private enterprise and formulating and enforcing minimum standards to prevent exploitation and injury, the promotion of the general welfare in this country requires that our government, sometimes, perform certain economic functions which are unprofitable to, or beyond the scope of, or deemed unsuitable for private enterprise. (Providing for national defense, police and fire protection, public health measures, education, transportation and other public utilities, conservation programs, highways and the postal system, for example.)*

(g) Has some understanding of the main features and principal effects and defects of the various governmental measures for sustaining farm income which have been attempted or proposed, and is studying this problem.

Developmental Equivalents for 3.43

(Expectations for younger or less mature students)

Is beginning to understand that many of the services rendered to children are being transferred from the family and the neighborhood to larger institutions of the community, and that these services have to be paid for from taxes.

Understands how government services are financed.

Examines various proposals for improving housing conditions in the nation and supports those which he believes most effective for the purpose.

Learns about those things which the government provides, such as hospitals, postoffices, national forests and parks, etc.

Begins to sense the danger to our world and to the future, of waste in the expenditures of natural resources.

207

Learns about the provisions and reasons for such activities as zoning, fire protection, public housing, and community planning in the community.

Learns the different ways of getting and using power, and how it is distributed and controlled.

Begins to understand that the depletion of natural resources; the waste of human resources through preventable illness, unemployment, or lack of education; the obsolescence of productive equipment; and the failure to renew or to advance productive "know-how" will result in a lower level of living in this or any other country.

Studies the resources of the state and nation and how they are used, the waste of resources, government assistance, and pertinent laws.

Observes regulations while camping, traveling in national parks, etc.

Is becoming acquainted with practical problems in relation to agriculture, erosion, conservation, fire protection, wildlife.

3.44 Sensing the Principal Problems Involved in the Operation of Our Economic System and Revealing an Interest in Maintaining and Expanding Its Values.

3.441 Knows the merits of the free enterprise system compared to other ways of organizing economic life and supports it as the dominant system in American economic affairs.

Illustrative Behaviors

(a) Accepts changes in ideas and practices made necessary by changing social and economic conditions.*

(b) Understands that advances in levels of living are made possible by the investment of savings in education and research to provide men with new knowledge and improved skills; in the accumulation of better and more productive equipment (capital); and in the opening up of new natural resources and the better use or renewing of those presently in use.*

(c) Evaluates the strengths and limitations of the American capitalistic system.

(d) Knows that the ultimate purpose of our economic system is to produce and to distribute as many and as much as possible of the goods and services which our people want in order to maintain a high standard of living, and accepts this as his basic criterion for making judgments regarding our economic life.

ORGANIZATION OF PROPOSED OUTCOMES

(e) Compares communism, socialism, fascism, and capitalism in terms of how they encourage and reward individual initiative and creative energy.

(f) Evaluates the various economic systems in terms of their
accomplishments and potentialities for providing a high
standard of living for the greatest number of people.

(g) Understands and compares the place of private enterprise and private ownership of property under capitalism, socialism, communism, and fascism.*

(h) Recognizes that the goal of our nation is a high level
of living widely distributed within a framework of maximum freedom for the individual, but that the goal in a
communist state seems to be the perpetuating in power
of the ruling elite, with concessions in respect to providing for general economic well-being made only as they
are necessary to keep the workers productively at work.

(i) Knows about and can use data afforded by the reports of
the gross national product, national income, and personal income to throw light on the overall success of our
economy; to note changes in our level of living; to make
himself aware of changes in the character and relative
importance of the different kinds of goods and services
being produced; and to estimate what these imply
about his own and the nation's economic welfare.

(j) Recognizes that private ownership of property is basic
to our economic system; that individuals are generally
free to buy or sell such property; and that the government sets up and enforces regulations so that exploitation of, or injury to, others is as far as possible prevented.*

(k) Has reached at least a tentative position with respect to
the advantages and disadvantages of the free enterprise
system on the basis of his study of the alternatives and
sees the need to guard against its abuse.*

(l) Is able to discuss some of the principal issues of organization, management, and control of production, distribution, and consumption of goods and services in a
technical age.*

(m) Studies the changes that the past fifty years have shown
in the nature of consumer goods and in manufacturing,
and in the nature of employment.

(n) Has some understanding of different opinions concerning the role of government in relation to business and
industry; begins to formulate some principles upon
which decisions on this matter should be made from
time to time.

BEHAVIORAL GOALS OF GENERAL EDUCATION

3.442 Understands the need for wise management of money, credit, and capital under our economic system, and approves action by voluntary organizations and by government when necessary to ensure such management.

Illustrative Behaviors

(a) Understands the importance of capital to economic progress; recognizes that ownership of capital is widely dispersed in the United States and that this ownership carries social responsibility.

(b) Sees how banking and credit serve our economy.*

(c) Appreciates the protection the national government provides the public through insurance of bank deposits and through regulation and supervision of commercial banking systems by the federal reserve system.

(d) Recognizes how charts and graphs can be used to interpret economic trends and economic data, and can read the kinds ordinarily appearing in newspapers and popular magazines.

(e) Appreciates something of the impact of unemployment and overproduction on economic conditions.*

(f) Studies the rise and fall of stock prices, meaning of inflation, variation in individual incomes, and sees the effect of depressions upon individual and family incomes; and realizes the importance of a relatively stable economy.

(g) Understands the factors which cause inflation, depressions, and unemployment.

(h) Understands something of the relationship of business enterprise to availability of money, full employment, public confidence, and demand for goods.

(i) Has an elementary understanding of the operation of business on borrowed capital and the need for regulations to limit credit and establish appropriate rates of interest.

3.443 Is sensitive to the advantages of both "big" and "little" business in this country and favors public policies which keep both functioning in our economy.

Illustrative Behaviors

(a) Recognizes the advantages to the public of big business, such as efficiency of mass production methods, technological progress through research, patent laws, control of raw material supplies, and advantages inherent in volume of purchase and sales.

(b) Is aware of some of the unethical practices and subterfuges sometimes used to hamper the "small" merchant in the free operation of his business and is forthright in supporting honest business practices.

(c) Is informed on the role of the farmer in both the American and world economy; recognizes that some farmers are "small" businessmen while others are "big" businessmen.*

(d) Sees something of the issues involved in farm legislation.

(e) Favors efforts to develop national and state farm policies which are fair to "small" and "big" farmers and to consumers of farm products.

(f) Understands the sources of the power of industry and business and the responsibility of industrialists, stock owners, and businessmen to use this power properly.

Developmental Equivalents for 3.44

(Expectations for younger or less mature students)

Studies the economic differences between capitalism and communism.

Discovers how money came into use as the result of the division of labor and the exchange of goods.

Contrasts barter and money in making purchases.

Is becoming familiar with labor organizations and problems when and as they affect his immediate area.

Learns something of the chief types of American unions and their patterns of organization.

Gains appreciation of the part that labor force has played in making America strong and prosperous.

Begins to recognize the power which labor unions as a pressure group have in American politics.

Is able to explain something of the role of management in manufacturing and other enterprises.

Recognizes the effects of collective bargaining on wage levels.

3.45 Recognizing the Problems Related to Organized Business and Organized Labor; Being Sensitive to Both the Uses and Abuses of These Rights.

3.451 Recognizes the functions to be served by industrial organizations (workers and management) and approves of the exercise of their rights and the assumption of their responsibilities in our economic life.

Illustrative Behaviors

(a) Recognizes right of both management and labor to organize freely—business in associations and corporations under state charters; labor in unions, etc.

(b) Has some understanding of the principal labor problems and tries to be increasingly fair and objective in

BEHAVIORAL GOALS OF GENERAL EDUCATION

looking at the problems involving labor, management, and the general welfare.*

(c) Has begun to discover the importance of various labor-management groups, or of organizations with which affiliation might be desirable; e.g., knowledge of labor unions, health insurance groups, retirement.*

(d) Has learned to evaluate labor or professional organizations carefully and plans to join those organizations most valuable to him, and to use them for his own good and that of his fellow workers.

(e) Advocates public employment on the basis of merit without prejudice as to race, religion, or national origin.

(f) Has visited, or read about, and so understands something of the operations of a large industrial organization, and of a large labor organization.

(g) Recognizes some of the monopolistic practices of management, of labor unions, farm organizations, etc., in the principal forms in which they occur.

(h) Understands the meaning and operation of collective bargaining, mediation, and arbitration as these are practiced in this country; opposes the premature and unnecessary use of strikes and boycotts and of violence in labor-management controversies.*

(i) Has some understanding of the role of labor unions in our economy. Knows the approximate extent to which workers are organized into unions in this country and the chief reasons for the development of unions.

(j) Recognizes the social responsibility of labor and expects to assume responsibility for the action of any labor group to which he may soon belong.

(k) Thinks critically about rights and obligations of different groups and about what constitutes an appropriate share of productive resources to employer, employee, and stockholder groups.

(l) Disapproves action of organized labor when the general welfare is disregarded; favors a "cooling-off" period in such situations.

(m) Participates with others in helping to raise the standards of performance in his chosen occupation or the basic protections of his career.

(n) Begins to identify some of the factors which contribute to a worker's economic problems: lack of basic education, lack of opportunity for adult education related to his job, increasing demands of technology, automation, housing, illness, etc.*

ORGANIZATION OF PROPOSED OUTCOMES

3.452 Recognizes the need for legal control of activities of organized industrial groups and for protection of these groups and their members.

Illustrative Behaviors

(a) Has some knowledge of employment restrictions, discrimination, opportunities, and protection imposed by or offered by trade unions, business organizations, professional associations, state examining boards, and by labor legislation.*

(b) Supports legal measures which protect the rights of labor to organize and to work for good working conditions, and which recognize the right of every individual to compete for any job for which he is qualified.*

(c) Supports the cause of free labor, but exercises critical judgments on methods used to secure ends.

(d) Expresses himself freely in supporting the elimination of discrimination in employment.

(e) Recognizes need to resist unfair demands of labor leaders on business and the general public and for legal machinery for meeting such demands.

(f) Recognizes prejudicial legislation, and resists it when in a position to do so.

(g) Is sensitive to the economic problems faced by certain special classes of workers (itinerant labor, minority groups, child labor, etc.) and uses his influence to ensure by law fair employment and labor practices and wholesome conditions of work.

(h) Has some understanding of the more important existing legislation affecting employer and employee relationships.*

Developmental Equivalents for 3.45

(Expectations for younger or less mature students)

Learns something about modern business organization, labor unions, government regulations and consumer problems.

Studies the contributions of labor and management.

Seeks answers to questions pertaining to disagreements between management and labor.

Reads about unions and their purposes and how they operate.

Begins to understand the justification for, and purposes of, labor unions and of the responsibilities he faces as a prospective union member for proper use of union power.

PLAN FOR EVALUATING A PROGRAM OF GENERAL EDUCATION

At some future time we may have instruments that will evaluate the developing maturity of students in each of the four areas of competence and with some reliable data on rates of growth toward maturity in each of the three directions upon which this study is based. It is possible now, however, for a high school to make some worthwhile evaluations of its program of general education in terms of the students' behavioral competence if it obtains and studies the judgments of teachers who are most familiar with the school's program, of laymen in the community who are most familiar with its high school youth, and of senior students who have experienced its program. It is probable that some consensus as to the strengths and weaknesses of the program will appear and, on the basis of these judgments, discussions can be launched which will result in constructive suggestions for program improvement.

Two kinds of judgments ought to be sought from each participant in such an evaluating effort. First, each should be asked to indicate how important he thinks it is for the high school's general education program to attempt to increase students' behavioral competence in a particular way. For example, the participants might be asked whether a high school should help students make a wise choice of life-work. Second, each participant should be asked to indicate how well satisfied he is with the effort the school is making through its general education program to help all its students achieve competence to do this. Wherever there is a consensus that a particular type of behavioral competence is important, but that the school is not now making much effort to develop it, a point has been discovered where program improvement is in order. These judgments, when they represent the pooled beliefs of persons who are in a position to have knowledge of the situation being studied, make a sound basis for action.

The evaluative form which follows has been designed to provide an opportunity for groups of teachers, laymen, and students to express their ideas concerning the importance of each of the behavioral outcomes included in this study as an element in the general education program of their high school, and also to express an opinion as to how much effort they think the school is now making to develop the competence the outcomes require. A given school will be more likely to use this form a section at a time rather than as a whole because schools usually work only on one or two problems in general education at a time—health education, for example. In such an instance a school would use only the sections of the evaluative form dealing with health. If a school wants to make an overall evaluation of its general education program, then it would use the whole form.

The form makes it possible to rate either an item's importance or the school's effort, 5 indicating a high rating and 1 a very low one. It also provides a zero to be used where a participant does not think the behavior ought to be sought by the school at all, or where it is desired to register the opinion that the school is making no effort to stress it. Intermediate ratings of 2, 3, and 4 are also provided. Some preliminary discussions of the plan of evaluation by those who are to participate and of the possible results of its use will probably increase interest and understanding of it and lead to better results. By tabulating the results of the independent ratings of the teachers, laymen, and senior students, interesting agreements and disagreements can be discovered and a basis for curriculum discussion, study, and improvement created. Additional copies of this form for use by such groups may be purchased from Russell Sage Foundation, or sections of it may be duplicated by any local school as needed.

FORM FOR EVALUATING GENERAL EDUCATION PROGRAMS IN TERMS OF BEHAVIORAL OUTCOMES

WHAT BEHAVIORAL OUTCOMES SHOULD OUR HIGH SCHOOL STRESS?

Information: This form is designed to help you express your opinion on two things: (1) How important do you think it is for this high school to seek to affect student behavior in each of the ways appearing on the following list? and (2) How satisfied are you with the effort the high school is making in its general education program to affect this behavior? (A high school's general education program is generally agreed to consist of the subjects all are required to study and its student activity program which is open to all.)

Instructions: To register a very strong or favorable opinion you should check an item in the column under the figure 5 on the form. To register a very weak or unfavorable opinion, you should check an item in the column under the figure 1. If you think the item should not be in the list at all or that the high school is doing nothing about it, you should check the item in the column under the zero. The page numbers refer to pages in Part III.

Example: Your form should look like this when you have expressed your opinion of each item:

How important is it?

5	4	3	2	1	0	
☑	☐	☐	☐	☐	☐	To help students make a wise choice of life-work.

How satisfactory an effort is the high school making?

0	1	2	3	4	5
☐	☐	☐	☐	☐	☑

These checks show that you consider this to be very important and that in your opinion the high school is making a very satisfactory effort. Rate each of the following items *in these two ways:*

1. GROWING TOWARD SELF-REALIZATION.

1.1 Developing Behaviors Indicative of Intellectual Self-Realization.

1.11 Improving His Study Habits, Study Skills, and Other Work Habits.

1.111 Is skillful in securing information and in organizing, evaluating, and reporting results of study and research. (Pages 92 to 93)

1.112 Displays an inquiring mind: is intellectually curious and industrious. (Pages 93 to 94)

1.113 Can learn independently and shows desire to do so. (Pages 94 to 95)

1.114 Recognizes the importance of continuing to learn. (Page 95)

Developmental Equivalents for 1.11 (Expectations for younger or less mature students). (Pages 95 to 96)

How important is it?

HIGH		LOW			
5	4	3	2	1	0

How satisfactory an effort is the high school making?

LOW				HIGH	
0	1	2	3	4	5

1.12 Improving in His Ability to Communicate Ideas and to Recognize and Use Good Standards.

    1.121 Commands and uses the basic skills of reading for information, ideas, opinions, stimulation, and leisure. (Pages 96 to 97) -------→

    1.122 Expresses his ideas in speech, writing, or in some artistic form with increasing clarity and correctness. (Pages 97 to 98) -------→

    1.123 Demonstrates his command of quantitative thinking. (Page 98) -------→

    1.124 Is developing some artistic and literary tastes and standards; exhibits creative capacity in some form of worthwhile intellectual activities. (Page 99) -------→

    Developmental Equivalents for 1.12 (Expectations for younger or less mature students). (Pages 99 to 100)

1.13 Becoming Sensitive to, and Competent in, the Use of Logical Thinking and Problem-Solving Processes.

    1.131 Tends to make an objective approach to a problem and attempts to define it clearly. (Page 100) -------→

    1.132 Seeks pertinent information and organizes and evaluates data. (Page 101) -------→

    1.133 Recognizes logical and illogical thinking in his efforts to reach reasonable conclusions. (Pages 101 to 102) -------→

    Developmental Equivalents for 1.13 (Expectations for younger or less mature students). (Page 102)

1.2 Developing Behaviors Indicative of Growth Toward Cultural Orientation and Integration.

1.21 Revealing the Personal Understandings and Characteristics of the Good Citizen.

    1.211 Understands the meaning of basic democratic values. (Page 103) -----→

    1.212 Practices basic democratic values. (Pages 103 to 104) -----→

    Developmental Equivalents for 1.21 (Expectations for younger or less mature students). (Page 104)

1.22 Attaining a Perspective on Present-Day Events, Cultures, and Conditions.

    1.221 Develops a sense of historical time and of cultural perspective. (Pages 104 to 105)-----→

    1.222 Senses the problems and issues facing us in relationships with other peoples in the world. (Pages 105 to 106) -----→

    Developmental Equivalents for 1.22 (Expectations for younger or less mature students). (Page 106)

How satisfactory an effort is the high school making?

LOW 0 1 2 3 4 5 HIGH

How important is it?

HIGH 5 4 3 2 1 0 LOW

1.23 Attaining Orientation to the Physical World and Appreciation of What Scientific Advancements Mean to the World.

1.231 Shows some evidence of developing an intelligent and understanding relationship between himself and the physical world. (Pages 106 to 107)— — — — — — — — →

1.232 Grows in ability to apply scientific fact and principle. (Page 107)— — — — — — — →

Developmental Equivalents for 1.23 (Expectations for younger or less mature students). (Page 108)

1.24 Improving in Ability to Apply Ethical Values as Gained from Religion, Philosophy, and Direct Experience to His Own Decisions and Behavior.

1.241 Makes an effort to relate value systems to his own and to others' conduct. (Page 108)— — — — →

1.242 Examines his own conduct and tries to improve it. (Page 109) — — — →

Developmental Equivalents for 1.24 (Expectations for younger or less mature students). (Pages 109 to 110)

1.25 Developing Aesthetic and Artistic Appreciations.

1.251 Shows growing enjoyment of the creative arts and participates in aesthetic and artistic activities. (Page 110)— — — →

1.252 Shows growing ability to appreciate and apply good standards of performance and artistic principles. (Pages 110 to 111) — — — →

Developmental Equivalents for 1.25 (Expectations for younger or less mature students). (Pages 111 to 112)

1.3 Developing Behaviors Indicative of Growth Toward Personal Mental and Physical Health.

1.31 Improving in Understanding and Control of Emotional Self.

1.311 Becomes more self-reliant and independent; seeks to identify and control fears and worries. (Pages 112 to 113) — — — →

1.312 Shows increasing emotional stability. (Pages 113 to 114) — — — →

Developmental Equivalents for 1.31 (Expectations for younger or less mature students). (Page 114)

1.32 Improving in Understanding and Control of Physical Self.

1.321 Views his body and its functioning objectively and scientifically. (Pages 115 to 116) — →

1.322 Is learning to live and work within physical and mental health limits and to recognize signs of poor health and physical strain. (Page 116) — →

Developmental Equivalents for 1.32 (Expectations for younger or less mature students). (Pages 116 to 117)

1.33 Showing Intelligent Use of Accepted Health Practices, and Wise Action on Health Problems.

1.331 Is increasingly self-directive in care of his health. (Pages 117 to 118) — →

1.332 Takes intelligent action on his health and hygiene problems. (Pages 118 to 119) — →

Developmental Equivalents for 1.33 (Expectations for younger or less mature students). (Pages 119 to 120)

1.34 Making Intelligent Use of Accepted Safety Practices.

1.341 Recognizes importance of safety practices and obeys rules and regulations. (Page 120) — →

1.342 Practices highway safety—as car-driver and pedestrian. (Page 121) — →

1.343 Has first-aid skills. (Page 121) — →

1.344 Is prepared to help meet community health and safety emergencies. (Pages 121 to 122) — →

Developmental Equivalents for 1.34 (Expectations for younger or less mature students). (Page 122)

1.4 Developing Behaviors Indicative of Growth Toward Economic Literacy and Independence.

1.41 Preparing to Make Intelligent Choice of Life-Work.

1.411 Surveys the world of work as a step in choosing his career. (Pages 122 to 123) — →

1.412 Studies his own physical and mental capacities and interests as he surveys occupational opportunities and what they provide and demand. (Page 123) — →

1.413 Begins to make a deliberate choice of preferred types of life-work on the basis of reason and judgment and to prepare for it in high school. (Pages 124 to 125) — →

Developmental Equivalents for 1.41 (Expectations for younger or less mature students). (Pages 125 to 126)

221

How important is it?

HIGH 5 4 3 2 1 0 LOW

How satisfactory an effort is the high school making?

LOW 0 1 2 3 4 5 HIGH

1.42 Becoming a More Efficient Worker Through Actual Work Experience.

1.421 Seeks actual work or other first-hand experience for practice of skills and for observation of conditions in the fields he is considering. (Page 126) →

1.422 Develops good work habits and attitudes toward work and seeks to acquire desirable personal qualities. (Page 127) →

Developmental Equivalents for 1.42 (Expectations for younger or less mature students). (Pages 127 to 128)

1.43 Becoming a More Intelligent and Economically Literate Consumer.

1.431 Recognizes importance of considering quality, price, and actual need when buying, and knows how to get reliable information. (Pages 128 to 129) →

1.432 Takes proper care of equipment, clothing, food, and other products for which he is responsible. (Page 129) →

1.433 Is informed and competent in the handling of money. (Pages 129 to 130) →

Developmental Equivalents for 1.43 (Expectations for younger or less mature students). (Pages 130 to 131)

1.44 Manifesting Intelligent Understanding of Our National Economic Life and Institutions.

1.441 Recognizes the free enterprise system as a dominant factor in American economic life. (Pages 131 to 132) →

1.442 Recognizes need for taking personal interest in, and responsibility for, conservation of natural resources. (Pages 132 to 133) →

Developmental Equivalents for 1.44 (Expectations for younger or less mature students). (Page 133)

2. GROWING IN ABILITY TO MAINTAIN DESIRABLE SMALL (FACE-TO-FACE) GROUP RELATIONSHIPS.

2.1 Developing Behaviors Indicative of Intellectual Growth and Development.

2.11 Manifesting Acceptable Family Membership.

2.111 Maintains understanding relationships with parents and other family members. (Pages 134 to 135) →

2.112 Participates in family activities and does his share of work around the home. (Pages 135 to 136) →

2.113 Is beginning to anticipate the possibility of having a home of his own some day. (Pages 136 to 137) →

Developmental Equivalents for 2.11 (Expectations for younger or less mature students). (Page 137)

222

2.12 Sustaining Friendly Contacts with One's Friends and with Others in Small Unorganized Groups.

2.121 Has friendly attitudes toward others and ability to accept them as individuals. (Pages 137 to 138)

2.122 Is developing character qualities and command of social courtesies and skills needed in interpersonal relationships. (Pages 138 to 139)

2.123 Improving in his ability to communicate in conversation with, and in writing to, another (personal letters—furnishing information or giving directions). (Pages 139 to 140)

Developmental Equivalents for 2.12 (Expectations for younger or less mature students). (Pages 140 to 141)

2.13 Developing Behaviors Indicative of the Kinds of Competence Needed as a Member of Small Organized Groups.

2.131 Joins organized groups when their purposes relate to his tastes and interests, and develops the personal characteristics which contribute to successful small group membership. (Pages 141 to 142)

2.132 Helps to plan group activities and does his share in carrying out plans. (Page 142)

2.133 Works well with others while maintaining his own views, ideas, and standards. (Pages 143 to 144)

2.134 Uses democratic values and practices in organized group activities and in relations with fellow members. (Pages 144 to 145)

Developmental Equivalents for 2.13 (Expectations for younger or less mature students). (Pages 145 to 146)

2.2 Developing Behaviors in Small Group Situations Indicative of Cultural Orientation and Integration.

2.21 Improving Understandings and Attitudes Which Facilitate Desirable Relationships Within the Family.

2.211 Recognizes importance of the family as a social institution. (Pages 146 to 147)

2.212 Appreciates opportunities for cultural and intellectual activities within the family. (Page 147)

Developmental Equivalents for 2.21 (Expectations for younger or less mature students). (Pages 147 to 148)

223

2.22 Adopting Cultural and Social Amenities Required in Contacts with Friends and Others in Small Unorganized Groups, and Desirable Interpersonal Attitudes and Skills in Processes Needed in Such Groups.

2.221 Displays in serious, but informal, small group discussions, the interests, knowledge, and techniques needed for acceptable participation. (Page 149)

2.222 Uses organized group activities as a means of developing artistic, creative, social, and political interests and abilities. (Page 150)

Developmental Equivalents for 2.22 (Expectations for younger or less mature students). (Pages 150 to 151)

2.23 Utilizing Various Kinds of Competence Needed by Members of Small Organized Community Groups.

2.231 Is especially careful to apply the principle of full respect for personality toward small community subgroups when they represent cultural, racial, and religious interests different from his own. (Pages 151 to 152)

2.232 Exercises as a student interested in civic and political affairs, or as a junior member of such groups in the community, the civil rights to which he is entitled, defends them for others, and assumes the responsibilities of a young citizen. (Pages 152 to 153)

2.233 Is actively interested in the problems faced by the school and community, and works in appropriate ways as a member of the student body and of community groups. (Pages 153 to 154)

2.234 Understands the role of religious organizations and of other organized groups with social service, or ethical interests and programs; and joins them or otherwise expresses his constructive interest in their efforts in his community. (Pages 154 to 155)

Developmental Equivalents for 2.23 (Expectations for younger or less mature students). (Pages 155 to 156)

2.3 Developing Behaviors Involved in Maintaining Physical and Mental Health and Safety in Small (Face-to-Face) Group Situations.

2.31 Maintaining Health in the Home.

2.311 Does his share to contribute to physical health and safety in the home and family situation. (Pages 156 to 157)

2.312 Tries to maintain and promote family mental health. (Page 157)

Developmental Equivalents for 2.31 (Expectations for younger or less mature students). (Pages 157 to 158)

2.32 Maintaining Health as a Participant in Small Peer-Groups.

2.321 Recognizes need to maintain physical health in small peer-group situations, and contributes toward its attainment. (Pages 158 to 159) - - - →

2.322 Begins to recognize need for, and to contribute to, mental health in small peer-group situations. (Pages 159 to 161) - - - - - - - - - →

Developmental Equivalents for 2.32 (Expectations for younger or less mature students). (Page 161)

2.33 Contributing to Health and Safety in Small Group Situations in School and Community.

2.331 Recognizes importance of community safety programs and facilities, and cooperates in their maintenance and development. (Page 162) - →

2.332 Recognizes the need for community control of health conditions. (Pages 162 to 163) - - - - - - - - - - - - →

Developmental Equivalents for 2.33 (Expectations for younger or less mature students). (Page 163)

2.4 Developing Behaviors Indicative of Growth Toward Economic Competence and Independence in Small Group Situations.

2.41 Improving Economic Competence and Independence in Family and Small Group Situations.

2.411 Participates and cooperates in family financial matters. (Pages 164 to 165) - - - - - - - - - - - - - - - - - →

2.412 Recognizes need for being an economically intelligent member of the family and of small groups to which he belongs. (Page 165) - - - - →

Developmental Equivalents for 2.41 (Expectations for younger or less mature students). (Page 166)

2.42 Becoming a Good Member of Work-Groups.

2.421 Is concerned that groups exercise care in economic matters. (Pages 166 to 167) - - - - - - - - - - - - - - - - →

2.422 Begins to recognize and assume the rights and responsibilities of members of work-groups. (Pages 167 to 168) - - - - - - - - - →

Developmental Equivalents for 2.42 (Expectations for younger or less mature students). (Pages 168 to 169)

225

2.43 Manifesting Interest and Participation in the Economic Affairs of the Community.

2.431 Holds some opinions on economic affairs of the community and its organizations and institutions based on his study of them. (Page 169)

2.432 Takes an interest and participates in groups concerned about the community's use, management, and conservation of its natural resources. (Page 170)

Developmental Equivalents for 2.43 (Expectations for younger or less mature students). (Page 170)

3. GROWING IN ABILITY TO MAINTAIN THE RELATIONSHIPS IMPOSED BY MEMBERSHIP IN LARGE ORGANIZATIONS.

3.1 Developing Behaviors Indicative of Intellectual Growth and Development.

3.11 Becoming Intellectually Able to Follow Developments on the World and National Levels and to Formulate Opinions About Proposed Solutions to Some of the Principal Problems and Issues.

3.111 Is developing an interest in, and understanding of, world events, conditions, and organizations. (Pages 171 to 173)

3.112 Endeavors to become well informed on the backgrounds of the larger problems of our nation and the world and to make an intelligent analysis of the issues involved. (Pages 174 to 175)

Developmental Equivalents for 3.11 (Expectations for younger or less mature students). (Pages 175 to 177)

3.12 Identifying Himself with Large Groups and Organizations Interested in Cultural, Social, Economic, and Political Affairs, and Becoming an Effective Member of Them.

3.121 Is an intelligent and active member, at least on a "junior" level, of large groups and organizations. (Pages 177 to 178)

3.122 Exercises rights and duties in political organizations when permitted, and gains increasing understanding of democratic policies and procedures. (Pages 179 to 180)

3.123 Has some understanding of the way public opinion is formed; uses defensible methods in helping to form it; and guards against being victimized by the indefensible methods of others. (Page 181)

Developmental Equivalents for 3.12 (Expectations for younger or less mature students). (Pages 181 to 182)

3.13 Evidencing Intelligent Appreciation and Support of Democratic Goals and Principles and of American Cultural, Social, and Political Traditions.

3.131 Appreciates and respects democratic goals and principles and political traditions in American life. (Pages 182 to 184) — — — — — — →

Developmental Equivalents for 3.13 (Expectations for younger or less mature students). (Pages 184 to 185)

3.2 Developing Behaviors Indicative of Growth Toward Cultural Orientation and Integration.

3.21 Viewing Current Events and Conditions in This Country and in the World in the Light of Their Historic and Cultural Pasts.

3.211 Is able to relate some principal world problems and situations of our day to events and conditions of the past. (Pages 186 to 187) — — — — — →

Developmental Equivalents for 3.21 (Expectations for younger or less mature students). (Pages 187 to 188)

3.22 Developing Cultural Background Through Reading and Participating in Various Cultural Organizations and Activities.

3.221 Reads and uses other means of communication to expand his knowledge and appreciation of his own and other cultures. (Page 188) — — →

3.222 Is interested in, joins, or supports a few organizations of various types as a way of getting a variety of cultural experiences and appreciations. — — — (Pages 188 to 189) — — — — — — — — — — — — — →

Developmental Equivalents for 3.22 (Expectations for younger or less mature students). (Page 190)

3.23 Seeing Vocational Activities in Their Cultural Settings.

3.231 Recognizes his chosen life-work not only as a means of support but as his way of making a contribution to his country and the world. — — — — — (Pages 190 to 191) — — — — — — — — — — — — — — — — →

Developmental Equivalents for 3.23 (Expectations for younger or less mature students). (Page 191)

3.31 Developing Behaviors Indicative of Understanding Problems of Mental and Physical Health.

3.31 Recognizing Health as a World Problem, and Supporting Worldwide Scientific and Humanitarian Efforts and Organizations.

3.311 Supports various worldwide organizations working to improve world health conditions and standards. (Pages 191 to 192) — — — — →

3.312 Understands the roles of research and political action in solving public health problems. (Pages 192 to 193) — — — — — — — — — →

Developmental Equivalents for 3.31 (Expectations for younger or less mature students). (Page 193)

How important is it?

HIGH 5 4 3 LOW 2 1 0

3.32 **Appreciating and Supporting Work and Services of Federal, State, and Local Health and Safety Departments, and of Volunteer Organizations.**

3.321 Appreciates and supports work of federal, state, and volunteer agencies in the field of public health. (Pages 194 to 195)

3.322 Is constructively interested in and supports organized community health and safety programs and activities. (Pages 195 to 196)

3.323 Supports organizations and programs designed to provide highway safety and to prevent accidents and disasters in the community and in industry. (Page 196)

3.324 Recognizes the importance of mental health and the needs of the physically handicapped, and takes an active interest in such matters. (Pages 196 to 197)

Developmental Equivalents for 3.32 (Expectations for younger or less mature students). (Pages 197 to 198)

3.4 Developing Behaviors Indicative of Growth Toward Economic Competence and Independence.

3.41 **Recognizing the Worldwide Application of Economic Principles and the Economic Interdependence of the Peoples of the World.**

3.411 Recognizes interrelation of human welfare and economic life, and supports programs and organizations designed to recognize and act on these facts. (Pages 198 to 199)

3.412 Knows something about the varying economic resources of different areas of the world, the different levels of productive ability, and the resulting standards of living; and sees the necessity for developing economic conditions and relationships which take these facts into account. (Pages 199 to 200)

3.413 Recognizes the responsibilities of United States for leadership in settling world economic problems and favors federal government programs designed to meet these responsibilities. (Pages 200 to 201)

3.414 Sees world trade as a means of promoting the economic welfare of the United States and of other countries, as a means of preventing war, as a way of promoting cultural interchange; and favors policies which promote world trade. (Pages 201 to 202)

Developmental Equivalents for 3.41 (Expectations for younger or less mature students). (Page 202)

3.42 **Supporting Measures of Federal, State, and Local Government, and Voluntary Organizations Designed to Conserve Human and Natural Resources.**

228

3.421 Believes in the conservation of human and natural resources, practices it, and supports programs and organizations concerned with this → national problem. (Pages 203 to 204) – – – – – – – – – – – – →

Developmental Equivalents for 3.42 (Expectations for younger or less mature students). (Page 204)

3.43 Understanding the Need for Federal and State Governments' Stimulative and Regulatory Activities in Economic Matters and Affairs as Means of Making Our Free Enterprise System Work.

3.431 Supports the principle of individual economic freedom which the free enterprise system is designed to provide and favors governmental activ- → ity designed to ensure the operation of this principle. (Pages 205 to 206) →

3.432 Recognizes that there are situations and occasions when it is necessary and wise for federal, state, or local government to enter a productive activity, although it supports the principles underlying the free enter- → prise system. (Pages 206 to 207) – – – – – – – – – – – – – – – →

Developmental Equivalents for 3.43 (Expectations for younger or less mature students). (Pages 207 to 208)

3.44 Sensing the Principal Problems Involved in the Operation of Our Economic System and Revealing an Interest in Maintaining and Expanding Its Values.

3.441 Knows the merits of the free enterprise system compared to other ways of organizing economic life and supports it as the dominant system in → American economic affairs. (Pages 208 to 209) – – – – – – – – →

3.442 Understands the need for wise management of money, credit, and capital under our economic system, and approves action by voluntary organizations and by government when necessary to ensure such → management. (Page 210) – – – – – – – – – – – – – – – – – – →

3.443 Is sensitive to the advantages of both "big" and "little" business in this country and favors public policies which keep both functioning in our → economy. (Pages 210 to 211) – – – – – – – – – – – – – – – →

Developmental Equivalents for 3.44 (Expectations for younger or less mature students). (Page 211)

3.45 Recognizing the Problems Related to Organized Business and Organized Labor; Being Sensitive to Both the Uses and Abuses of These Rights.

3.451 Recognizes the functions to be served by industrial organizations (workers and management) and approves of the exercise of their rights and the assumption of their responsibilities in our economic life. → (Pages 211 to 212) – – – – – – – – – – – – – – – – – – – →

3.452 Recognizes the need for legal control of activities of organized industrial groups and for protection of these groups and their members. (Page 213) →

Developmental Equivalents for 3.45 (Expectations for younger or less mature students). (Page 213)

229

SELECTED BIBLIOGRAPHY

SELECTED BIBLIOGRAPHY

This bibliography has been developed for the use of the members of a local school system's staff who are directing and participating in the improvement of a high school's curriculum, but with special reference to its general education program. For orientation to such work it includes some items supplying background on secondary education in America, and on the secondary school program in general. It includes some items dealing with general education in college if they also have relevance for the high school and others which deal specifically with the theory and practice of general education at high school level.

AIKIN, WILFORD M., *The Story of the Eight-Year Study*. Harper and Bros., New York, 1942.

ALBERTY, HAROLD B., *Reorganizing the High-School Curriculum*. Macmillan Co., New York, 1953, chaps. 1–8.

ALEXANDER, WILLIAM M., and J. GALEN SAYLOR, *Secondary Education: Basic Principles and Practices*. Rinehart and Co., New York, 1950, chaps. 12, 13, 15, 16.

ALLPORT, GORDON W., *Becoming: Basic Considerations for a Psychology of Personality*. Yale University Press, New Haven, 1955.

AMERICAN COUNCIL ON EDUCATION, *The Evaluative Criteria*. Washington, 1950.

ANDERSON, VERNON E., PAUL R. GRIM, and WILLIAM T. GRUHN, *Principles and Practices of Secondary Education*. Ronald Press Co., New York, 1951, Parts 1 and 2.

ANDERSON, VERNON E., *Principles and Procedures of Curriculum Improvement*. Ronald Press Co., New York, 1956.

ASSOCIATION FOR SUPERVISION AND CURRICULUM DEVELOPMENT, *What Shall the High Schools Teach?* National Education Association, Washington, 1956, chap. 5.

BILLS, ROBERT E., *About People and Teaching*. Bureau of School Service Bulletin, vol. 28, no. 2, 1955. University of Kentucky, Lexington.

CASWELL, HOLLIS L., editor, *The American High School* (John Dewey Society Eighth Yearbook, 1946). Harper and Bros., New York, 1946, chap. 7.

COLE, LAWRENCE E., and WILLIAM F. BRUCE, *Educational Psychology*. World Book Co., New York, 1950, chap. 2 and Part 2.

COREY, STEPHEN M., and others, *General Education in the American High School*. Scott, Foresman and Co., New York, 1942.

DODDY, HURLEY H., *Informal Groups and the Community*. Bureau of Publications, Teachers College, Columbia University, New York, 1952, chap. 1.

DRESSEL, PAUL L., and LEWIS B. MAYHEW, *General Education*. American Council on Education, Washington, 1954.

ECKEL, HOWARD, *An Experiment in Teaching Educational Administration*. Bureau of School Service Bulletin, vol. 28, no. 1, 1955. University of Kentucky, Lexington.

EDUCATIONAL POLICIES COMMISSION, *The Purposes of Education in American Democracy*. National Education Association, Washington, 1938.

FAUNCE, ROLAND C., and NELSON L. BOSSING, *Developing the Core Curriculum*. Prentice-Hall, Inc., New York, 1951.

FEATHERSTONE, WILLIAM B., *A Functional Curriculum for Youth*. American Book Co., New York, 1950.

FRENCH, WILL, J. DAN HULL, and B. L. DODDS, *American High School Administration*. Rinehart and Co., New York, 1957, chaps. 3, 9, 10.

GENERAL EDUCATION IN SCHOOL AND COLLEGE: A Committee Report by Members of the Faculties of Andover, Exeter, Lawrenceville, Harvard, Princeton, and Yale. Harvard University Press, Cambridge, 1952.

GILES, HARRY H., S. P. McCUTCHEN, and A. M. ZECHIEL, *Exploring the Curriculum*. Harper and Bros., 1942, chaps. 1–2.

THE HARVARD COMMITTEE, *General Education in a Free Society*. Harvard University Press, Cambridge, 1945.

JOHNSON, B. LAMAR, *General Education in Action*. American Council on Education, Washington, 1952, chaps. 1–2.

KEARNEY, NOLAN C., *Elementary School Objectives*. Russell Sage Foundation, New York, 1953.

LEONARD, J. PAUL, *Developing the Secondary School Curriculum*. Rinehart and Co., New York, 1953, chaps. 4–11, 13, 14.

McConnell, T. R., editor, *A Design for General Education*. American Council on Education, Washington, 1944.

McConnell, T. R., and others, "General Education," *Encyclopedia of Educational Research*, edited by Walter S. Monroe. Macmillan Co., New York, 1950, pp. 489 ff.

National Society for the Study of Education, *General Education:* Fifty-First Yearbook, Part 1. University of Chicago Press, Chicago, 1952. *Adapting the Secondary School Program to the Needs of Youth:* Fifty-Second Yearbook, Part 1. University of Chicago Press, Chicago, 1953, chaps. 7, 12, 14.

President's Commission on Higher Education, "Establishing the Goals," *Higher Education for American Democracy*. Government Printing Office, Washington, vol. 1, 1947; and Harper and Bros., New York, vol. 1, 1947.

Saylor, J. Galen, and William M. Alexander, *Curriculum Planning for Better Teaching and Learning*. Rinehart and Co., New York, 1954, Parts 1, 2, 3.

Sharp, George, *Curriculum Development as Re-education of the Teacher*. Bureau of Publications, Teachers College, Columbia University, New York, 1951.

Shaw, Archibald B., and John L. Reid, "The Random Falls Idea," *The School Executive*, March, 1956, pp. 47–86.

Smith, Eugene R., Ralph W. Tyler, and others, *Appraising and Recording Student Progress*. Harper and Bros., New York, 1942, chaps. 2, 6, 10, 11.

Smith, B. Othanel, William O. Stanley, and J. Harlen Shores, *Fundamentals of Curriculum Development*. World Book Co., New York, 1950, Part 4.

Snygg, Donald, and Arthur W. Combs, *Individual Behavior*. Harper and Bros., New York, 1949.

Wynne, John P., *General Education in Theory and Practice*. Bookman Associates, New York, 1952, Introduction and chaps. 1 and 2.

Wright, Grace S., *Core Curriculum in Public High Schools*. Bulletin no. 5, U.S. Office of Education, Washington, 1950.

Core Curriculum Development: Problems and Practices. Bulletin no. 5, U.S. Office of Education, Washington, 1952.

"Core Curriculum: Why and What?" *School Life*, February, 1952.

INDEX

INDEX